Hidden Codes of the Universe

Uma Bhardwaj

First Published in April 2023

ISBN: 978-93-5741-542-2

BLUEROSE PUBLISHERS
www.BlueRoseONE.com
info@bluerosepublishers.com
+91 8882 898 898

Cover Design:
Muskan Sachdeva

Typographic Design:
Pooja Sharma

Distributed by: BlueRose, Amazon, Flipkart

Contents

The Dream

(In the year 2050, on planet Earth, India,)

Camille School of Modern Science is welcoming a new batch of students just like every day. The conference hall is large, with almost 100 students entering the class one by one. A big screen is displaying a scanning process with data feed for an e-scorecard. The students take their cards and make their way to their seats in the class. Slowly, the crowd is increasing in the hall. All students are seated, and the teacher, Kain is looking at them. She starts the class with a long "hello....

Kain: Welcome everyone, today you are going to be introduced to your parallel world partner for the first time. Until now, some of you may have unknowingly connected with each other at parties, but now you can connect with your parallel partner with caution. Before that, we need to understand some rules and basics of that world. You will only have access to your partner when they are unconscious. At that time, you can do anything, such as changing their state of mind, experiencing a new experience through their body, and so on. However, never forget that your partner should remain alive. Our world is directly connected to that world. Never forget this.

During her lecture, an emergency signal came on her smartwatch that was tied to her wrist. She stopped in the middle and said that someone else would continue the lecture in her place. She suddenly left the class, went to the gallery to look at Torrent, and asked if this was true.

Torrent says that 'nobody' is in a female body and she is in a parallel world. The software is in the year 2022 model.

Kain: does she know what it is and does she remember?

Torrent: no ma'am. All activities are very ordinary.

Kain: what is their time now?"

Torrent: few worlds are very close in time. Chances are high that she will land on Earth at the same time as Kashkashian University.

Kain: but why are you showing concern about it?

Torrent: every value system matches with that world.

Kain: you know what it means, Torrent. We need clarity at any cost.

On November 24, 2021, Upasana Center in Lucknow.

(Upasana meditation is one of the most ancient spiritual practices in India, in which a practitioner must remain in silence in the meditation center for 10 days.)

Aparna wakes up in the morning and on the sixth day at 4:00 am, she hears the bell in the Upasana meditation center. Aparna wonders where she is and if it was just a dream. She finds it strange that such a dream would come from meditation or maybe it was a result of the continuous silence.

Aparna goes to the bathroom. She looks at herself in the mirror and takes a deep breath. She wonders if there is a place that is so technologically advanced that it cannot even be seen by us. But she decides not to dwell on these thoughts. She has come here to clear her mind, focus, and relax. She needs to go back to Delhi to look for a new job. She thinks to herself that the next bell will ring at 4:30.

Aparna lifts her torch and heads towards the meditation hall. In the meditation hall, all the seats are fixed in place beforehand. She goes to her spot, sits down, closes her eyes, and waits for the instructions for the meditation. Then the audio starts. The guru guides them to focus on the sensations in their body. Pay attention to the entire body. Do not let any part slip away. The flow of the current from top to bottom, bottom to top.

As she keeps listening, Aparna gets lost in meditation. There are no thoughts in her mind. Her attention is only on the sensations in her body.

Present Day

1st January 2022, Delhi, India.

Aparna is packing up with her husband Vijay. She is very happy today because she is shifting to her preferred new home from C Block Janakpuri, Delhi to A Block, Paschim Vihar. She has been thinking about it for so long and finally, she has got her dream 2BHK flat. She has already done the whole interior design in her mind.

She has always enjoyed interior design. All the household items within 15 days Vijay and Aparna have recently made new purchases. A new sofa set, a 55-inch LED TV, and all the kitchenware were bought according to Aparna's preference. Aparna has also created a small garden in the balcony of the house. Both come home from the office in the evening and have tea snack parties. Occasionally, they sit at the nearby Dhaba to eat famous Delhi-style malai chap and tikkas.

Now, she has also landed a new job. She has joined Future Bright Insurance Company as a branch manager. For the first time, Aparna is very happy with her life and feels now it will become perfect. When she goes to the office, she is fully focused and working diligently. She is also building a new team and has hired five people.

Ankur and Sudhir are quite active among them. Most of Aparna's office time goes with them as both are very active in the field. Aparna and both are hitting the sales target of the entire team together. Working seems like a party every day. When the three of them go out on a sales call, the entire office knows that they will come back only after closing the deal. As soon as they returned, both qualified for the Goa contest. Aparna is enjoying her work.

It is a cold day, yet Aparna wakes up at 5:00 am and leaves for field calls at 7:00 am. January, February, and March are considered the most important months in the insurance industry. Aparna earns the most incentives during these three months. Waking up early in the morning to go to the field has become a routine for her. Coming home at night early and meditating has now become a luxury. Aparna no longer has time for her side business, the 'Bodhi meditation center.'

The first week of February has arrived and there is a new sales target and a new contest launched in the office. Like every day, Sudhir and Ankur come to Aparna's desk with excitement.

Sudhir says that there are four-five meetings scheduled in the Faridabad Road, Mathura, Raya area, where we do not have any branch, so cross-selling there will be easy.

Four-five deals will be closed at once. Aparna, as always, gets ready for joint field call support.

Eating Bhang

As usual, Vijay drops Aparna off the next day at the Piragadi Delhi where Ankur and Sudhir were waiting. A new journey begins.

The first meeting is held at 9:00 am on Faridabad Road, and the deal is closed right away. All three are very happy. Ankur and Sudhir open their tiffin boxes, take different varieties of snacks, and sit at a tea shop to discuss the next meeting while having breakfast.

Around 1:00, they arrive for the second meeting, which does not close. Now they come out and look for a roadside eatery for lunch. They find one on the highway and discuss the third meeting while eating. The third meeting is near a village close to Mathura and it ends. After this meeting, the next meeting is with a school teacher who asks them to meet him in the market. Ankur, Sudhir, and Aparna are looking at each other's faces, and they all know it is a meeting regarding a person named Nitin Aparna, will not be fruitful but Aparna still says that let's complete this one last meeting for the day.

They park the car in the market and meet with the client at a local chaat shop. As usual, Sudhir introduces Aparna to the client with a 5-minute act, exaggerating her qualities. Seeing this, the three of them quietly laugh at each other. Instead of saying she is the branch manager, he always says, "Sir, this is our Aparna madam. She is the head of this entire zone, and we are here on a tour. We've come to you with a solution to any issues in your existing policy."

And The solution to any issues in your existing policy has now come to you by coming here on this tour.

Together, these three form an excellent team, each playing their designated role based on their mutual understanding. They communicate so well with each other that they can convey their thoughts through eye contact alone in front of the client.

After the meeting, it is already around 7:30 pm, and they decide to visit a nearby Shani temple. They all agree to this casual plan, and whenever they go out for meetings, they explore famous eating places, and tourist spots, or enjoy window shopping while walking.

As they walk, Aparna, as usual, video calls Vijay, sometimes showing him the quiet path of the temple, sometimes the jungle, and sometimes the temple. It is Aparna's habit to share everything with Vijay. They are also good friends with each other's spouses. At the temple, Sudhir and Ankur meditate with Aparna. They return to the nearest city, Mathura, and look for a hotel. While having dinner, they plan for the next day's meetings in Mathura and the surrounding villages.

The next morning, Aparna gets ready and knocks on Sudhir and Ankur's door.

As always, there is playful banter between Sudhir, Ankur, and Aparna.

Aparna: "Come on, let's get ready and go. Let's have an adventure on the way."

Ankur: Ma'am, let us have breakfast and then leave. We do not know much about the meetings ahead, there are two or three meetings, but the people from the village do not give a fixed time.

Aparna: Yes, that is right. Let us see if we can find some good local breakfast here.

Three people are going by car towards the market side. Then Sudhir's eye falls on a roadside stall-like place, where many local people are having breakfast - jalebi, khasta kachori, samosas. All three get down and have breakfast. Sudhir says, "Madam, we had a great breakfast for three people for ₹100. It was enjoyable."

Aparna responds, "Yes, absolutely. It is both cheap and tasty. Now tell me, where do we have to go from here? Did you get the location from the client?"

Ankur: Yes ma'am, there is a location and a landmark, it's a 40-minute drive from here. It is called Raya Village.

The three of them head toward their meeting, passing through fields and narrow alleys until they finally reach the client's house. They each know their role.

Sudhir's job is to introduce Aparna to the client so that the client thinks that a high-ranking officer from Bright Future Life Insurance Co. has come, and whatever she says will make him a millionaire today.

Aparna's job is to understand the situation and the client's financial condition and give presentations accordingly.

Ankur's job is to complete documentation and remind Aparna about the product and ticket size in between so that the product with the highest weightage is obtained when the deal is closed.

In between, they never miss keeping a personal connection with the client, sometimes they have food at the client's house, and sometimes they go with the client to roam around the village.

On that day, the client offered a sweet lassi to drink. And they went to visit the temple built by the client's ancestors. On the way back, he even showed the driver the way.

All three were happy and the deal was closed. They had to come back to Mathura for the next meeting. While joking and laughing, all three were moving ahead in the car. Meanwhile, Aparna saw a government shop selling 'bhang' written on a signboard from the left side window.

Upon seeing the signboard, it is not clear what happened to her. Suddenly, she stopped the car and said, "Brother, today I want to try bhang, and after consuming it, I will meditate." At first, Ankur and Sudhir hesitated a little, but Aparna was insisting in a way that made them think they had to take it.

Sudhir: All right ma'am, we will look. If it is your wish, then let's get off and buy it, and then we'll come back.

There, Aparna encountered a monk and a pandit purchasing bhang, a cannabis-infused drink. Curious, she inquired about their purchase and was informed that it is an offering to Lord Shiva and referenced in the Atharvaveda as Vijaya. When used in moderation and with proper intention, it can aid in meditation. After conversing with them, Aparna decided to purchase some fresh bhang and took a small portion before leaving in her car.

Ankur: how did you like it, madam?

Aparna; it tasted like mehndi. I do not think there's any high in this grass-like chutney. You were scaring me for no reason.

Sudhir: why did you want to eat bhang, madam? .... You meditate so much and even teach meditation, where did all these things come from in your mind?

Aparna: I do not know about that…. Yeah man, ……why did I have bhang? Hmmmm…. I think on the tenth day of the Upasana meditation, there is a state called the "bhang state" during meditation. …Maybe …they put this in my mind…. they said some kind of mantra in the Pali language that day and Pali is one of the world's oldest languages. …So maybe unconsciously, the seed of bhang came to my mind from there. Anyway, it does not matter… I am not feeling anything new; you know I just want to try it I thought it will help me to deepen my meditation.

Sudhir: you are making us fool mam; we feel like you must have had it before.

Aparna: Bhai, you must have understood by now that I don't have anything useless to hide. If I had eaten it, would I be ashamed in front of you guys? No..not at all.

By the way, why were you guys scaring me and saying that it is a dangerous thing?

Ankur: because Madam, I had eaten it once and my health had deteriorated. I had taken an oath to never touch it again in my life.

Aparna: never mind. Nothing happened to me. Sudhir, tell me about the details of the next meeting. What are the details?

Sudhir: Madam, there is not anything special in the fund value in the existing policy, but it seems like a big opportunity to discuss. Let us see what we can get out of it after we go and have a look.

Ankur was driving while Aparna was sitting in the front passenger seat, and Sudhir was sitting in the back seat. Almost half an hour had passed. Green fields stretched out on both sides. Aparna was looking at the greenery of the fields when suddenly Sudhir's voice came from behind, "Madam, look at the peacock!"

Aparna's ears echoed with a strange sound. She looked at Sudhir in surprise.

Aparna: What was that?

Ankur: What happened, Madam?

Aparna: What's going on, guys? Why are your voices coming in slow motion? How am I hearing my own voice? Are you guys hearing it correctly?

Ankur and Sudhir burst out laughing.

Ankur: Madam, you were talking about grass and now you got lost in it.

Aparna: oh my god… what's happening, How can the wind pass through the ears like this? What is happening, my hands and feet are not feeling anything.

Sudhir: Madam, are you okay?

Aparna: everything looks strange, what did I eat? …. The same road is appearing in two different ways, almost 50 meters ahead, ..aaaa…there is a hazy mist like a water bubble, ..and in front of it is a clear road, we are walking in the foggy net…. One bubble burst. Now we have entered the second one. What is happening? …Why did the car suddenly slow down?

Ankur: Ma'am, the car's speed did not slow down, it's just that you're feeling that way. That is why we were refusing, but you are very stubborn and do not listen to us.

Aparna: how long will this go on, ……. please fix it., (in few seconds) What happened, you all look normal again.

Sudhir: Madam, you may insist like a child, but the experience is also something, I am at least 10 years older than you. Now tell me, if Vijay Sir calls in such a situation, what should we say?

Now you are responsible for us.

Aparna: brother, it was a mistake ....so give the lecture later and now you need to tell me how to fix it.

Ankur: it is okay, do not worry... everything will be all right soon.

Look, we will fix it in the morning. We will stop somewhere on the highway and buy a salty lassi, yogurt, or lemon water.

Ankur gave a tense look to Sudhir and said "She will not be able to make it to the next meeting."

Aparna: You idiots..., you are still worried about meeting.... are you getting me what I am saying? ... I do not understand anything... It seemed like nothing had happened in five minutes and now it is getting strange, like conscious and then unconscious. And when I am unconscious here, it feels like I have reached another world.

I do not know how to explain it. ... Oh god I just want to be normal.

Ankur: mam, some people permanently reach the other world and never come back.

Aparna: ohh man, talk normally. First, something is wrong with me already, now you are talking like this...see I am not feeling my hands and feet.... oh god...am I going to die...

(It is almost like an hour passes like this.)

That day, Aparna realized for the first time that our five senses can lie to us. There is much more to the world than what we can perceive through our senses, and it is essential to keep an open mind and be aware of the limitations of our sensory experience.

After reaching home, she told Vijay that a strange day passed.

Changes in Perception

Aparna researched this thoroughly. She also felt that after this day, she becomes more sensitive in her attention. Now she understood that the plant had increased her perception. She understood that there is something else besides these five senses - seeing, hearing, touching, taste, and smell, which she should know.

A few days later, Aparna sat in meditation at night. After a short while, she experienced a sense of Samadhi. She continued to practice Yogic sleep that night and eventually fell asleep. It was the first time she had experienced conscious sleep. The next morning, she suddenly woke up screaming and said, "No, I don't believe it." Vijay also woke up upon hearing her voice and asked her what had happened. Aparna replied, "I don't know, I don't remember. It felt like I was talking to someone like an angel or god all night in my dreams."

Vijay said, "hmmm very good (in sarcasm). ...you know when somebody eats that type of substance ...bhang, etc.. Then these things happen.

Your strange things and these. Experiments with meditation.... I do not know where you get these crazy ideas from. If you had married a Haryanvi boy from Haryana, you would have known."

Aparna: if you had married your ex-girlfriend instead of me, you would have found out as well.

(Both of them laugh and then Aparna gets up to make tea).

Aparna now started giving time to meditation again. Whenever she got a chance, she would practice meditation. She did not use any mantra or worship any deity during meditation. She only focused on observing her own breath and body sessions. After 10 days of silent meditation, now she feels normal to be alone in silence.

Welcome Mother-in-law

One day, Aparna and Vijay were drinking tea together as usual, and then Vijay's mother called and told them that she was coming to Delhi from Odisha for a relative's wedding and would be staying with them for a few days.

Aparna feels both happy and worried upon hearing this. She is happy because her relationship with her mother-in-law has improved and they enjoy spending time together. She wants to take her to Delhi's local markets for shopping, eating, and hanging around but it will be difficult to find time during the peak season of the insurance industry. However, Vijay is not aware of this.

Aparna prepares for her mother-in-law's arrival by making collages of her photos from her mobile phone, ordering a cake, and making flower bouquets. She also prepares breakfast in the morning, although she herself must go to the office, so she leaves after getting everything ready.

Vijay brings his mother home, and Aparna's surprise is well-liked by her mother-in-law.

In the evening, Aparna returns home and meets her mother-in-law, asking about her experience in the new house.

They have a lot of conversations between them, and they enjoy dinner together with everyone at night

Now there had been some changes in Aparna's routine.

She was trying to take full responsibility for her mother-in-law but always felt guilty that the old woman might be cooking her own food in the afternoon.

It had been a week. Aparna now felt like she is being judged by her mother-in-law for everything. She starts, judging her office timing, her clothes, food and drink, everything.

She also had heard conversations between her mother-in-law and sister-in-law many times. When she was alone, she tried to explain her point of view to her mother-in-law with her best effort but somehow, she fails every time. Everything was going on like this.

Aparna's office routine was also getting more hectic than earlier.

On top of that, one day, she was a little upset and wanted to discuss these things with Vijay but as she started the conversation Vijay said to her that "she is doing everything for herself, not doing a favor for anyone. Many females work and manage their homes and take care of their children, but what are you doing separately?"

Aparna felt very bad hearing this. She could not even argue with Vijay in front of her mother-in-law.

As usual, she separated herself a little and started meditating. She did not enjoy her office that day and missed a field meeting. She felt an empty feeling inside, even though she could not figure out why. She did not even feel like going home. There was an old habit of hers, that whenever she felt a little deficient from within, she would go out for a walk. But it was not possible this time.

The Feelings which Invite Meditation

After 2-3 days, her mother-in-law asked her to visit Mathura, Vrindavan, and Haridwar. Aparna thought that maybe this would give her the opportunity to spend some time alone with her mother-in-law. Another side she was worried about his new office as she should not take leave and her bank account was also almost empty due to changing houses, but she manages somehow and still planned a trip with her mother-in-law.

In the last week of February, she left with her mother-in-law.

Aparna takes good care of her mother-in-law and talks to her like a friend. She really likes it when her mother-in-law tells her where they will go next while they are traveling. Last time when she was with her group of friends at this same place, they talked about old stories.

One evening, Aparna and her mother-in-law came back to the hotel after sightseeing.

Her elder sister-in-law call to her mother, speaker of the phone was so loud that Aparna was able to hear everything,

The sister-in-law said, "Mother, why did you go out alone like this? It's tense, there's no one there who can take care of you. You should go with a responsible family member who can take care of you" Aparna was listening to all of this. Hearing this, her expression changed. She kept thinking about how much she wanted to bring her mother-in-law here with her heart. She felt very bad after hearing this. She got upset she thought at least she should speak with Vijay about it so she called Vijay, but she found out that he was sitting at home with a friend. She thought she should not disturb him.

So, she went out alone for a while. She sat at a tea shop outside. She did not take her mobile phone with her, she just wanted to sit with herself for a while.

Aparna craved solitude and took the opportunity to sit with her thoughts. As she sipped her tea, a series of questions flooded her mind. "What am I doing? What do I truly desire from life? Why do I feel a sense of emptiness within me?" The weight of these questions brought tears to her eyes as she reflected upon her life.

She questioned whether she was merely running away from her problems and why she could not seem to find inner peace. Doubts crept in, wondering if she was doing something wrong and if her efforts went unnoticed. She pondered the idea of needing recognition for her good deeds and why it's challenging to understand those closest to us. Amidst these musings, Aparna wondered if perhaps she was overthinking the situation.

"Perhaps I have grown overly sensitive lately. Small things seem to affect me more than before. Maybe it is due to the increased financial burden since getting married. I feel like I am failing to meet my in-laws' expectations of being the ideal daughter-in-law. I struggle to wear a saree and my cooking doesn't compare to theirs. It's a stark contrast from my own home, where I'm known for cooking the best food. But I've been running the household since the beginning of my marriage, and that's just how it is. I'm in control of my own decisions, which is why Vijay and I live together in Delhi. If I had married someone from Haryana and had to live with my entire family, I would not have been able to pursue my career or achieve what I have.

Speaking of my career, I have been promoted six times in just under five years and earned more than my colleagues who started with me. I travel frequently and have won more awards than my age. So, what is the problem? Why do I find myself trying meditation, listening to spiritual speakers, and craving solitude? I remind myself of how far I've come, from studying in a Hindi school in the village to where I am now. Yet I cannot help but wonder if my life would be different had I married someone other than Vijay."

Lost in thought, she finishes her tea and take a deep breath before heading back to the hotel.

Her mother-in-law was lying in bed

Aparna asks, "Mother, how are you feeling?"

She replies, "I'm feeling good." Both talk for a while and fall asleep.

Two days later, they left for Haridwar.

In the evening, it is time for the Ganga Aarti (prayer). At the Haridwar ghat, the temple bells ring, the sound of the Aarti can be heard, the scent of incense fills the air, and the sun sets. Many people sit by the Ganges shore.

Aparna enters every Har Ki Pauri with her mother.

Mother-in-law: We'll have to take off our shoes at the shoe stall. There are a lot of crowds there.

Aparna: Don't worry, mother. Give me your slippers. Aparna takes out a plastic bag and puts her and her mother's slippers in it. She then signals to her mother and says, "Let's go, it's done."

Mother-in-law smiles and says, "At least you saved us half an hour." They both find a place on the stairs and sit down.

After a while, Aparna sits with her back straight in a cross-legged position. With her eyes closed, she begins to meditate.

Despite the noise around her, there is no disturbance at this moment. It is like nothing is needed at this moment. 15 to 20 minutes have passed.

She is only aware of her breathing, with no other thoughts or concerns. There is no pain in her body.

Everything feels empty. After a few moments, she opens her eyes and sees the flickering flames and floating lamps in the water. She realizes that her meditation today felt right, and there was no need to remove her attention from it. Her mind feels peaceful

At that moment, her mother-in-law asked, "Aparna, what are you meditating on? Are you reciting mantras or something?"

Aparna replied, "No, nothing like that. I was just sitting like this and feeling a sense of peace."

Her mother-in-law asked, "Still, there must be something you were focusing on, right?"

Aparna hesitated a bit and then said, "Shiva... I am meditating on Lord Shiva. He is my guru."

After saying this, she started to wonder herself, "Why did I say, Shiva? Why only Shiva and nothing else?"

After staying in Haridwar for two days, they left for Delhi by train.

Now, Aparna is sitting and meditating there on the train also. She sat on her seat for four hours with her eyes closed as if she had fallen into a deep sleep. Suddenly, her eyes opened, and she felt that her eyes were wet. Her breath was coming slowly, and as soon as she opened her eyes, she felt that her heartbeat had just started.

It felt like she was talking to someone. She must have felt some connection. She did not remember anything, just a feeling.

Aparna brought meditation back into her daily routine after coming back to Delhi. Things were not the same as they used to be. Now Aparna was thirsty for that same feeling. It became a common practice for her to sit alone and meditate after coming back from the office.

Eagle-The Invitation to a new journey

It was the month of March. There was a lot of work pressure from the office.

She also had the responsibility of her mother-in-law at home. Spending time with her mother-in-law was also important.

She often went shopping with her mother-in-law. She also had to send something for everyone when her mother-in-law went back home. Two little devils, Kittu and Vedu, were waiting for their Aunt Aparna to send toys and clothes for them. Aparna, along with her mother-in-law, bought something for everyone.

One day, Aparna was wandering around the nearby park during the evening, feeling angry about something. During those days, she also had a job offer from Dubai. She was thinking to herself that she should leave next month, as she wasn't able to do anything special here and maybe something good will happen if she goes there. While she was lost in thought, Aparna's mother called her and they were discussing the job offer.

Suddenly, an eagle flew above her head and placed its talons. She continued talking to her mother while telling her about the eagle. Her mother said that she would ask a priest and find out what it means, as it was a strange occurrence. Eagles do not just fly over someone's head like that.

After that day, for some unknown reason, Aparna's reactions become a bit more intense. Usually, she never used to react to certain things, but now she reacts very sharply to those same things.

Aparna has a playful nature, and her childhood always shines through in her behavior. But she only shows this childishness in front of her husband and her father. She speaks very sweetly.

Due to her easygoing nature and friendly demeanor, people around Aparna tend to share all their secrets with her. She is a little playful by nature and prefers to spend money rather than save it.

After the incident in the park, when Aparna realizes that there are changes happening in her nature every day, she starts consciously noticing her changes. One day, while watching some videos on the internet, she came across a video titled "What happens if an eagle sits on your head?" Upon seeing the title, she abruptly stopped the video and thought to herself, "These people are just showing ridiculous things to drive everyone crazy."

Then she starts another video, her favorite spiritual speaker Jagatguru.

"Jagatguru is not only famous in India but also around the world. He is a yogi, mystic, author, poet, divine seer, and internationally renowned speaker. He has many followers all over the world. Jagatguru is one of the top 10 most famous people in the world today. Aparna mostly watches Jagatguru's videos on her mobile or TV. Her thoughts always match his videos. Most of his concepts are such that Aparna feels like she is sitting there and speaking. Not only Aparna but also big actors, cricketers, and scientists are included in Jagatguru's fan list."

Due to Aparna's spiritual interests, she often ends up having arguments with her husband Vijay. Vijay tells Aparna every time to "save all these things for your old age. Why do you keep meditating so much?" Vijay believes that Aparna is beyond his understanding.

On the one hand, Aparna likes all adventurous activities such as paragliding, underwater diving, and similar activities. If it were up to her, she would spend her entire life just traveling around. She would jump off a mountain twice a day and when she sits down to meditate, she will remain completely silent for ten days.

Sometimes she becomes so relaxed that she does not feel bad about anything, and sometimes she becomes so emotional that if someone hits a street dog with a stick, she will fight with that person.

Nowadays, Aparna does not see the day or the night, neither the morning nor the evening. Whenever you see her, she seems to be lost in thought, as if some kind of research is going on in her mind, or she is reading a spiritual book, watching a video of a spiritual teacher, or meditating alone.

March has begun and Aparna's office has brought in a new target and a new contest. But this time, Aparna is not focused on her work. Vijay and his mother both feel Aparna's changing nature. Vijay has told Aparna several times that you are not normal these days. What has happened to you? Aparna just gives one answer - everything is fine, give me some time.

On March 16, 2022, like every night after dinner, Aparna went to her bedroom, and Vijay was looking at his mobile phone. Aparna said, "Vijay, please put on your earphones, I need to meditate.

Around 10:00 pm at night, Aparna sat down in meditation. Around 11:30 pm, Vijay fell asleep. Aparna could not sleep at all that night. Her focus and concentration were deepening as she only meditated, without reciting any mantras or the name of any deity.

She was just sitting there. Suddenly, she felt something round and rolling between her lower abdomen and back. She sat eagerly and watched what would happen. It felt like all the energy in her body was focused in one place, rotating, and rising towards her neck.

Sensations started coming into her neck. Her neck was also rolling and suddenly it jerked backward as if it would break. In less than a second, something flipped, something went up and something came down.

Suddenly, there was a picture in front of her closed eyes and she realized that in her previous life, she had left her body like this and she was the wife of a spiritual guru.

It took her less than a second to realize this, but tears had already flowed from her eyes so much that her entire t-shirt was soaked. This realization was so powerful that she even forgot to breathe.

She took a deep breath and then thought, "What was that?" She could not understand anything. She was feeling very light-headed in his body. She looked at the time and saw that it was four in the morning. She closed his eyes and went back to sleep.

The Confused Being

The next day, Vijay made tea and woke up Aparna at 8:00 in the morning. Vijay told her that she was in a deep sleep and he had been trying to wake her up since 7:00 in the morning. Vijay asked her what had happened.

Aparna hesitated and said, "I don't feel well, maybe." Vijay said, "You still have to go to the office... Are you going to go or take a day off today?"

Aparna couldn't take the day off as she had to go to the office. She sat down, confused about what to say to whom. She got ready for the office and felt a different kind of sensation that day. Her vision and hearing seemed clearer as if her ability to see and hear had improved.

Something must have happened last night. Her attitude towards her spiritual guru is changing, it seems.

She was feeling strange but did not speak to anyone.

Aparna reached the office. As usual, she need to register her entry with the office boy Jagat at the reception, and he asked for a pen. Then, she noticed that there were different perfumes, the smell of tea, and the smell of the dustbin in the office. She could filter out each smell and identify them. She wondered what was going on.

Suddenly, she noticed Jagat's confused face. Aparna saw that he had picked up and put down the register twice and the pen twice, unconsciously. This surprised her, and she asked Jagat, "What happened, Jagat?" Jagat looked at Aparna and said, "Madam, what happened? Take this pen and do the entry, what happened to me?

Aparna goes to her desk and updates her team on everyone's field meetings. The daily routine begins. That day, she notices that she is already saying the next sentence in her mind before people finish speaking. She does not understand what's happening. In the meantime, one of her team members, Jay, asks her about the John meeting. She cuts the conversation short and goes out into the lobby.

Aparna thinks to herself, "What the hell is going on with me?" She takes a deep breath and returns to her desk. She asks Jagat to bring her a glass of water and a coffee.

Aparna goes to her desk and takes updates on everyone's field meetings from her team. The daily routine begins. That day, she notices that she is already speaking the next sentence in her mind before people finish speaking. She does not understand what is happening. Meanwhile, one of her team members, Jay, asks her for the John meeting, and she cuts off the conversation in the middle and goes outside on the office floor, saying "leave me alone". Aparna wonders to herself, "What the hell is going on with me?" She takes a deep breath and goes back inside, asking Jagat to bring her a glass of water and a coffee at her desk. The whole day, everything in the office felt strange to Aparna. It seemed like either she had become a little faster or people had become a little slower. She felt that she had become more alert and sensitive than before. Above all, she kept remembering the meditation from the previous night

She comes home in the evening. Her mother-in-law is talking to her, telling her to make something special at home as tomorrow is

Holi. Aparna hears the words, but her attention is scattered. She tries to focus, but her attention is only on the sound, not the meaning of her mother-in-law's words. She notices that her mother-in-law's voice changes four or five times in a single sentence, and she can only focus on the voice modulation. She watches her mother-in-law without blinking, and notices every twitch on her face and every strand of hair in the rain. She had never noticed these things before. When her mother-in-law looks at her like this, Aparna feels something strange.

Aparna's mother-in-law speaks to her, "Aparna, are you okay? Are you listening to me?" Aparna feels strange about what is happening. She tries to be normal. Vijay sees her confused face and asks her what is wrong. Aparna does not understand what to say, so she says, "I'm not feeling well, maybe that's why I seem to like this

Aparna realizes that she has become very focused because of her continuous attention. She is happy with this, but seeing herself as a guru's wife, she is also surprised.

To clear up her confusion, Aparna searches for Jagatguru's wife on Google. She learns that when Jagatguru's wife passed away and entered mahasamadhi, Aparna was only seven years old. She also sees what has been written about Jagatguru's wife on the internet and what has been said about her in YouTube videos.

Aparna's personality matches that of Jagatguru's wife to a great extent. One place said that when Jagatguru went out for his events, she would keep an eye on him until he was out of sight. Aparna also does the same. She is emotional like Jagatguru's wife and, even at 32 years old, still has a lot of childlike innocence.

Sometimes, she becomes a serious seeker, and suddenly she becomes full of fun and mischief.

It is still not proven based on this that she is the deceased wife of the spiritual leader. Then Aparna also thought that the spiritual leader himself claims to be Tantric, he may have kept some tantra to help many people like me who have gone through a spiritual journey. Moreover, there are tantric things around Holi in our country. So, it is possible that many people like me have such experiences.

As Aparna was lost in her thoughts, suddenly Vijay came and said, "Let's go watch a good movie. Is this big TV just for show?" Aparna also thought it would be good to divert her mind for a while.

After watching the Hollywood movie "Interstellar," Aparna became confused because the concept of the movie was time dilation, which showed a black hole appears to slow down time. The movie depicted those 7 years on Earth is equal to 1 hour on another planet in terms of our perception of time. it is shown that time passes at different rates on different planets because of gravity. One hour spent on a planet near a black hole is equivalent to 7 years on Earth. This concept is known as time dilation and is a real scientific phenomenon predicted by Milstein's theory of relativity.

Aparna was also thinking why Vijay showed her this movie today. While thinking all this, Aparna was trying to sleep at night. But even though she was not sleeping straight, she was going straight into meditation without any effort. She remained in yogic sleep almost all night. Her body had become so sensitive that she could feel every breath, every pulse, and every nerve in her body throughout the night. Almost the whole night had passed before she could blink her eyes just a little while before morning. It felt like she had entered a dream while still awake. In the dream, a man spoke to her and said, "I have lived all my memories and now I just want to live in your memories. I want to learn from you, and I want to teach you something, please be with me."

Aparna feels quite strange when she tries to wake up from sleep. She woke up and looked at the clock, it was 5:00 in the morning. After that, Aparna did not try to sleep again. She lay back down with her eyes wide open and started thinking that perhaps she has been too obsessed with watching the videos of the spiritual leader, and it has affected her mind. Then she hears a voice from inside her and it says, "No, there is nothing like that." The voice was a completely different individual entity inside her. Aparna felt a little scared. She felt once that perhaps ghosts really exist and some ghost has entered inside her.

She remembers that Jagatguru had often said in his videos that the breath of those who meditate becomes very slow, and so the souls are attracted to their bodies. Aparna's breath had become much slower than before, and there was also a very large Peepal tree in the park near her house. So, Aparna thought that there might be a ghost inside her

Then she thought, even if there was a ghost, how could it show her someone else's face? Aparna couldn't understand. Just then, a voice from inside spoke, "I am not a ghost, you and I are one and the same. Just understand that I am a part of you."

Aparna was communicating with the voice without speaking.

In her mind, Aparna said, "What is happening? God, please make me normal." The voice replied, "You are already normal."

Aparna asked, "If I am normal, then what is happening to me, and who are you?"

The voice said, "I am the same one you were looking for." Aparna replied, "I was just meditating to stay calm."

Voice: It's not like that, that's the problem, in human beings, everyone lives in lies.

Aparna: So, you are a ghost.

Voice: I am not a ghost. But You cannot lie to me. I can know everything that you know.

Aparna: This is very strange. What should I call you? Who are you?

Voice: We are lovers from centuries ago.

Aparna: This is unbelievable. Is this really happening? It seems like I have done some wrong meditation. I was just doing worship and meditation. How did this happen? Have I gone crazy? This all does not seem normal. Who should I talk to about this?

Voice: Talk to me.

Aparna: (speaks loudly) not at all...

Vijay was sleeping beside her when he hears Aparna's voice.

Vijay: What happened to you? Early in the morning? Who talks like this? You are becoming a ghost day by day.

Aparna: Vijay, I think I need a doctor.

Vijay: First, show it to a doctor of the mind. You need a psychiatrist.

Aparna: Yes, I am also exactly saying that I should show it to a doctor of the mind.

Vijay: What happened? I am sorry. That was not my intention.

Aparna: No, I really need to see a doctor for the mind.

Voice: Just relax, give me some time. I will clarify everything. Why are you making a spectacle of yourself in front of your in-laws and husband here?

Aparna: Did you hear it? Did you hear it, Vijay?

Vijay: What did I hear? Did you have a bad dream?

Aparna takes a few seconds and tells Vijay that maybe she is not feeling well and she should take a day off today.

Vijay: Yes, it is okay. You take the day off. I'll tell mom to either bring food from outside or make something simple.

Aparna: It's not about the food. Anyway, I'm fine. I mean I'll make something myself. I just need some time.

Vijay speaks in a confused voice, "Yes, you can see for yourself, as you like it. I know you are worried, but mother will leave in a few days. Your birthday is on March 22, so I will book the ticket for a few days after that."

Aparna says, "Vijay, I don't understand you. It's not about that."

Vijay responds a little teasingly, "Yes mam, we are all crazy people who don't understand you."

The voice says, "That's true."

Aparna thinks to herself, "Be quiet."

Aparna says, "Vijay, please don't start now."

Vijay says, "Such a dirty expression in the morning. What should I make of it?"

Aparna says, "My expression is not in my control at the moment. Please support me, I am not feeling well inside."

Vijay says, "Your mood swings keep happening! ...I am also getting tired." Saying this, Vijay goes to the bathroom.

Aparna gets up and goes to the kitchen to make tea. She talks to herself about that voice.

Aparna: (talking with voice) Are you a spiritual guru? I've heard about Jagatguru many times in videos. They can leave their body and go anywhere."

The voice responds, "No, I am not the one you see on TV. But yes, you can consider me a Jagatguru or you can give me another name. I can easily explain everything to you at once. I have always been inside you, but due to your focus, your body has become very sensitive, and you are now able to feel me. What you experienced that night is your truth. Either you can also reject the truth altogether.

Aparna: I still do not understand, and why should I believe you? Why shouldn't I believe that you are a ghost?

Voice: Even if you believe that I am a ghost, I have been with you from the beginning. You will understand all of this after some time. First, think about where you are right now.

Aparna: I am in my kitchen. I am in Delhi, and in India.

Voice: Which Delhi?

Aparna: There is only one Delhi. I think you are trying to confuse me, don't you?

Voice: Give me some time, I will explain everything. This Delhi exists only in your mind. You think that there is only one Delhi, but everyone has their own Delhi in their mind.

Aparna: What do you mean?

After a while, Vijay comes to the kitchen and asks Aparna about the tea. Aparna: "It's ready, I'll give it to you in a minute." Aparna takes three cups of tea and sits in the drawing room.

She forgets to wish her mother-in-law a good morning. Both Vijay and his mother notice this

She is talking with that voice while drinking tea.

Voice: Let me explain with a simple example. You three are currently drinking tea. Do you think the color of the tea looks the same to all three of you? Does the color of the teacup look the same to all three of you? Does the taste of the tea also look the same to all three of you?

Aparna: I mean, yes, it looks the same. The tea tastes sweet and the color of the tea is just like tea. And the color of the cup is white.

Voice: I am not talking about color blindness.

It is also possible that two people may perceive the same tea as delicious in two different ways. This is an example of how our experiences and perceptions can differ even though we are part of the same world.

I am talking about the same color that you are calling white, Vijay also appears to be white, but both may or may not have a difference in white.

And also, is it the exact same taste that you feel coming to Vijay or your mother-in-law, can you guarantee this?

Aparna: Yes, you are right. I have never thought about it before. It is possible that I am seeing a completely milky white and Vishal may be appearing slightly less white.

And The taste I am getting from tea with tea leaves, ginger, milk, sugar, and water, the taste that Vijay is getting may be different.

But all these things do not prove that I am Jagat Guru's wife. And my question remains, who are you?

Voice: I told you that you can understand me according to your convenience. I just want you to understand whatever you can so that you can benefit from it.

After this, this conversation between Voice and Aparna continues.

She keeps trying to understand herself. Everything is fine. Aparna kept trying to understand all of this and kept thinking about her experience that night. She could feel from within that her inner feelings were changing for the Jagadguru. She did not talk to anyone. Now she wants to know the truth of her experiences in books or on the internet.

Vijay leaves for the office, after an hour Aparna closes her room from inside and sits down. Now she wants to understand and ask questions from that voice.

Aparna: yes, tell me, I don't want to confuse myself anymore. I want to reach a conclusion.

Voice: My job is not to lead you to any conclusion. Instead, I want to show you all the possibilities. I want you to draw your own conclusion. You want to know how it is possible that you were Jagat Guru's wife and you left your body in Samadhi. So, what are you doing here again? I want you to understand and know this from your own experiences, not just believe it.

First, you need to understand that we never die. We live in all possibilities. This entire world runs only on perception. All animals...all conscious beings are part of a big mind.

Do you remember when you were in the meditation center? There you had seen a dream on the sixth day. That dream is true. I had shown it to you...you had awakened me in meditation.

Aparna: all of this is happening in my mind. I mean, maybe there is nothing like this at all. Perhaps my mental balance has been disturbed.

Voice: Okay, calm down. I will make it easy for you. I will talk to you only when you want to talk to me. Or when you will look ready for further conversation.

Aparna notices all of this and wonders if it is possible that the effect of the bhang she had consumed in Mathura is still present. But then she thinks to herself, "No, that's not possible." It has been more than a month, and the effects of those things cannot last for so long. Then she tries to remember everything from the beginning and researches the plant on her own. While researching on the internet, she comes across some information.

'A woman named Priya Mishra is researching this plant. According to her research, cannabis or bhang, a type of plant, has been given great importance in ancient civilizations such as Greece, China, and Egypt, as well as in religions such as Judaism, Taoism, Buddhism, Sikhism, and Islam, and has been used as a medicine.

However, the oldest references to cannabis are found in India. In Hinduism, cannabis is considered Lord Shiva's offering and in India's ancient Ayurvedic medicine, it is considered equivalent to nectar. In Atharvaveda, it is described as one of the five most sacred plants on Earth, and more than 150 names have been given to it, such as Indrasan, Vijaya, Ajay, etc. Its mention is also found in Ayurvedic texts such as Sushruta Samhita, in which its medicinal properties have been analyzed. Cannabis or bhang is still used as a fundamental chemical in many Ayurvedic medicines.'

Aparna reads some books too. Her entire day goes by like this. She tries to sleep at night, but even unwillingly, she only stays in a state of yogic sleep. It is like she's talking to someone at night. Just before morning, she falls asleep.

The next day, when Aparna opens her eyes, Vijay was not in the room.

She gets up and checks the time and realizes it is already 10:00 in the morning. She thinks to herself, "Oh God, what's going on? Where am I stuck? While thinking all this, she goes out and sits on the sofa. She tries to remember what Vijay told her when he left, but her mind was not there. She does not even remember how she responded. Suddenly, she remembers her mother-in-law. She sees that her mother-in-law is making tea in the kitchen.

Aparna: Maa if you had woken me up, I would have made it.

Her mother-in-law does not respond. She has a smile on her face and is making tea. Aparna goes back to her room. She stands in front of the mirror.

Now she speaks. Oh God, what have I done to myself? I do not even remember when I wore clothes. Her hair is loose. Her eyes are swollen. She takes a rubber band and ties her hair first. She goes to the bathroom and washes her face and comes back to the kitchen. When she sees her mother-in-law, her mother-in-law was straining tea in a cup.

Aparna tells her mother-in-law, "Ma, I'm sorry. I am not feeling well these days. I am not able to concentrate on anything. "As she says this, she looks at her.

She saw her mother-in-law's face with just the same reaction, she just smiles, and her eyes don't even blink. Then her mother-in-law gives Aparna the cup of tea. And she just kept looking at her. Aparna felt a little strange. She takes the cup of tea and sits on the sofa in front of her. Aparna feels a little scared. But she did not say anything.

Then her mother-in-law says, "From this body, whatever possible help I can provide, I will do." Upon hearing this line, the mother-in-law becomes completely quiet. And now, the thought comes to her mind that this must be a definite fact, that there is a soul that was previously in her body and is now in her mother-in-law's body. She also understands that perhaps, it can happen because of meditation that night.

At the very next moment, her mother-in-law starts talking normally.

From that moment on, it happened almost every day. Sometimes she notices a change in breathing, and other times she sees a movement in Vijay. And the very next moment, they start talking normally. Now even for Aparna, it had become a common thing to see. She also noticed that when these activities happened, all the memories remained in the conscious memory of the people around her even afterward.

Three days have passed. Now the matter has reached a point where not only the internal voices, but also the external environment, videos playing on TV, and people around, all seem to be answering her questions.

Aparna kept watching all of this, experiencing it. When she slept, she was talking to someone, as if someone was trying to explain something to her. Every new morning, she woke up with new perceptions and conclusions! Aparna could not understand it.

She could not even able to work in his office. So, she left her job.

Her mother-in-law's ticket is booked for after two days. Vijay is also upset with Aparna.

He feels that Aparna was under work pressure and on top of that, her mother's presence at home is adding pressure. This is why Aparna is reacting this way. Aparna was not in a state to explain anything to anyone. The voice or soul inside her was scanning her memories, observing her.

Moving To The Hometown

During the day, when she sat alone, she talked as if Aparna was summarizing her entire life until now. All the conclusions of all the conversations are running inside her.

Sometimes that voice criticized Vijay and his mother-in-law, sometimes his job, sometimes his health. Sometimes she asked questions and got angry at Aparna, sometimes she expressed love and sometimes she made him feel proud.

On that day, that voice asked Aparna some very sharp questions. "What is your worth? Why are you doing all this? Do you consider what is between you and Vijay as love or compromise? Why do you keep so much in your mind? Why don't you tell anyone? What are you afraid of? What do you want from life?"

Here, you have nothing that you can call your own.

There were other things that had never occurred to Aparna. She had no answer to these questions. She did not understand anything.

That day, when Vijay came home, he insisted on going to Bhiwani (Aparna's hometown) Vijay wanted to stay in Delhi till his mother is here in Delhi, but Aparna could not understand and refused to comply.

Finally, Vijay had to listen to Aparna. That voice kept talking to Aparna repeatedly during this time.

Aparna: What does that mean? Are you trying to scare me even more now?

Voice: I am not scaring you, but I am showing you and learning something.

Vijay and Aparna leave in a hired car. The car moves forward like a Piragadhi from Paschim vihar.

Aparna was both scared and excited within herself. She sat quietly and looked out the window. Her window was on the right side, and the road on which the cars were crossing suddenly seemed to increase in speed.

After a while, what appeared from her window was like a TV screen. It was like someone had pressed the fast-forward button in a running movie. In about 30 seconds, many cars passed together. She saw that she was in the car in front of her. Sudhir and Ankur were with her. They were wearing the same clothes that they had worn in Mathura that day. After that, the speed was slowing down again, and the cars were moving. As soon as Aparna's car moved a little ahead from the Piragadhi Chowk, the speed became normal again. Aparna was just watching everything. Then on the right side, a crematorium appeared. Above the crematorium, a straight shiny white cloud-like thing appeared, which looked like a road.

Aparna was saying to herself, "I must have gone mad..."

Voice: not at all. How many things are there in your own world that you cannot see, but today you can see them, yet you are calling yourself crazy?

what Were you so curious to know? All the mysteries of the universe that you have been wanting to know for so many days are now coming to you openly. Why are you afraid?

Aparna now looks at the driver of the car. He is looking at his mobile phone with a map on it. Aparna's time is displayed on the map as 1 day, 4 hours.

Aparna asks the driver, "Brother, which map is this? We are going to Bhiwani, right?"

The driver replies, "Yes, madam. We will reach Bhiwani in one hour and forty minutes."

Aparna takes a deep breath and holds Vijay's hand, feeling relieved. Finally, both reach Aparna's home in Bhiwani. However, Vijay returns to Delhi with a heavy heart. He was also worried about his mother and Aparna. Aparna's family members were upset with Vijay for bringing her home so late.

Although Aparna feels a little better after reaching home, she still feels uneasy. After reaching home, she could not hear any sound. She also wanted to see a doctor herself.

The next day, Aparna's family takes her to the doctor. They go to Dr. Shoran, who is a famous psychiatrist. Aparna tells the doctor everything. After listening to everything, Dr. Shoran advises Aparna to get an EEG test. The EEG report comes back normal. Aparna's brother, Kamal, also talks to the doctor separately. The doctor tells him that Aparna may be under some kind of burden. Aparna needs rest for a few days. Any stressful topics should not be discussed in front of her. Aparna needs good food, a good environment at home, and proper sleep. Anyone who is close to Aparna in the house should try to talk to her openly about what is bothering her, if possible.

After coming home, Aparna starts taking her medicine. She sleeps almost the entire day and night because of those medicines. However, whenever she regains consciousness, her behavior is not the same as before. She talks to herself in between. She asks about her condition. She asks to sit in the sun. Sometimes she asks for water. Sometimes she asks for food to eat.

Aparna denies that voice. But she also knew that all of it was true, which she was hiding behind a curtain. Those were all the shortcomings in her life. The voice told her that all the questions she had asked were distressing for her.

In Aparna's family, her father is a retired army person, her brother is a chartered accountant, and her younger sister is married with a son. Her mother is a housewife. They shifted to Bhiwani city from a small village in Haryana about 10-11 years ago.

Bhiwani is one of the 19 districts in the state of Haryana and is filled with all the basic amenities. Bhiwani city is also called small Kashi because of its old temples where people come to worship. Most people here wake up early in the morning and start their day and go to bed early at night. There is no hustle-bustle like in big cities. The city has good schools, colleges, universities, markets, hospitals, cinema halls, and hotels. After returning home,

Aparna's family members try to ask her and find out what is bothering her. Everyone in the family is trying to figure out the cause of her illness according to their own perception. Some think it is because of continuously working, some think it is because of the hustle-bustle of Delhi city life, while others think it is because she did not marry a good boy.

Aparna always wanted to have a house with a courtyard. And a loving partner.

She wanted a career option that provided a regular income and allowed her to travel the world.

Like most houses in Haryana, Aparna's family also has ancestral lands, a house, a farm, and a plot. But Aparna does not feel entitled to any of it. In Haryana's culture, it is considered wrong for girls to claim ownership of their land. Girls are not considered co-owners of their ancestral property.

After completing her studies, Aparna went to Delhi NCR for a job. She pursued what interested her in marketing and sales. Her first job was at PolicyMarket.com in Gurugram, starting at ₹11,000. Then she worked night shifts as a BPO.

Aparna had a passion for traveling. Someone suggested joining the insurance industry, where they have international trips as sales contests. There would be incentives and opportunities to travel.

Then Aparna got an opportunity to work at the HBFC Life Insurance Company.

Aparna joined as an entry-level field sales officer here. She got promoted in six years and eight months. She also qualified for four international trips and once became the employee of the year. She won 36 trophies and held the position of Pan India number one. She took a rented flat and a car.

She was enjoying her life in installments. Sometimes she would party with her colleagues from the office, sometimes she would take a solo trip. Whenever she felt lonely, she would go to the mountains. Sometimes she meditated. However, the loneliness remained.

Her younger sister Seema had been married for two years. Her parents, relatives, and everyone were behind Aparna to get married, saying that everything would be settled after marriage.

One day, Aparna's father created her profile on a matrimonial website. Now he sends Aparna the photos and profile details of two to three boys every day. Aparna never paid attention to it.

It was August 2018 when she came to her home in Bhiwani. Her father said, "At least open your profile once and talk to some boys." Aparna also thought, "Maybe something good will happen if I talk to someone." She talked to the first boy, and after 15 minutes, she blocked him. She talked to the second boy. He was her husband, Vijay. He married her. The family was surprised again. When Aparna's parents asked why she liked Vijay, Aparna's answer was always the same. "He lets me be who I am."

Everyone lectured to Aparna. For marriage, everyone had to see the financial status of the boy's family. But Aparna never listened to anyone. Finally, Aparna and Vijay got married in April 2019.

But does life ever go straight? Slowly and gradually, the same pressure and emptiness came back to Aparna's mind. Now, she went to Dubai for work, transferred to Lucknow, sat in the meditation center Upasana, and went through different phases.

She could never stay away from Vijay and they were always together.

This time, Aparna's story took such a turn that she had to look at her life in a completely new way and think about it.

Now Aparna is with her family, leaving everything else behind. There has been a significant change in her demeanor. Everyone is tense. Despite taking medicine, her voice inside her is not suppressed. Instead, her voice has become so heavy that many times she responds as if she were Aparna. The medicine is of a heavy dose. Aparna's hands and feet are loose, and her tongue stutters many times. Now she wants to stop the medicine because of what she showed the doctor by thinking. It is not getting better, but rather the opposite effect is happening on her body.

According to the family members, she is sick because she is now responding rudely to everyone.

When Aparna's mother says, "You are in such a state because of your marriage. If you had a house to live in, this would not have happened. It is your in-laws' fault that they couldn't even provide you with a home after building one."

Aparna responds by saying, "Yes, Mom. It is not the fault of the one who gave birth to me and who has been discriminating between boys and girls since childhood. I've been in Delhi for so many years, and you've never worried about where I live or what I eat. Now that I am married, I'm so sick that even I can't come home. I have become a burden on you. You could not even give me a piece of land from all this property, but it is not your fault. Wasn't I born in this house?"

When her father says, "Daughter, you only got married because of your request. What did we do wrong? You had nine months' time before the wedding. What did you see? What did you test? What did you understand? I always said it is not for women. You should not work outside. You will feel like staying at home one day after leaving your job. Building a house is a man's job."

Aparna replies "Dad you worked in the army for so many years, and then worked in a private job in Okhla Industrial Area. If you would not be sold the land in the village, could you have built such a big mansion throughout his life in the city? which palace did he build? You are also a man, what happiness did you give to mom?"

Now when his brother Kunal speaks to him, he says, "What's the tension with you? Look, I am a CA and you are earning more than me? We are a middle-class family, everyone works, and it has been so many years since you started earning. Why don't you save? By now, you could have built your own house, you wasted all the money, you blew so much money."

In response to this, Aparna says, "You have grown up under the shade of your mother all your life.... Every night, when you felt like having milk, almonds, shakes, juice, or anything else, you kept ordering. .... Sitting at home and working from home, becoming the owner of all the property, and becoming the beloved son of the house, ...don't lecture me on saving money. ...Live my life for two days and see. When I roam in the field and forget the blisters on my feet. Even during my periods, I take the Delhi Metro and face the bumps. I go to people's homes and offices in the all-weather to sell insurance...do you even know ... How many times people look at me with those dirty eyes that I do not want. Sometimes I have to sit waiting for the bathrooms for two hours or more. I never eat home-cooked food myself, but if I cannot cook, then I am being judged for that.... All of this after being a soldier. ...My salary is in my hands. Yes, I cannot save anything because I am still alive from within. That is why I feel like traveling, sitting peacefully and eating good food, and shopping... Do not teach me what savings are. And as far as buying a house is concerned, why should I buy it? I also have a right to my father's land, on which I can make a claim one day. So, I will build my own house."

Now when Aparna's sister Sneha speaks, "you are so capable. you are independent. Now, this is not our home after marriage. Our home is our husband's home. Why do you fight with them? you should be fighting with your husband. Why don't you understand these poor people?"

Aparna says, "Yes, you are right. I am capable and you are a goat, right?... Tied up in an arranged marriage by your family. Yaa.... You have spent more than half of your marriage time here. Whenever you come, you take away the entire house with you. Every time you emptied the suitcase, all the beds and almirah. Your suit and saree are never complete.... The utensils, clothes, jewelry, makeup items, and even my belongings were taken away. ...Since the marriage, ... I have been watching these things.... Whom do you want to show by taking away these things from home?... And if you have a child now, it is also their mistake and your poor goat. .... What do you want from life? ...You do not have clarity. ...You do not know what you want from your husband. Didn't you have a choice to become independent? But you wanted to be a goat so that you could blame others. Have you ever tried to work hard on your abilities? Why did you take a course in fashion design? Have you ever focused on working for yourself? There is no poor person in this house. And if there is, then first see what you do with these poor people. You do not even see the pain of your mother's knees..."

Aparna had never spoken such harsh words to her family before. Vijay leaves his mother behind in Odisha and returns to Delhi. Despite Aparna's repeated refusal, the medication continues. Now Aparna does not feel like talking to her family. Sometimes when things quiet down, she feels sad inside. She does not want to say everything to everyone, but she cannot control herself.

Vijay has no idea about Aparna's condition. He wants to talk to her, but Aparna's family instead of arranging communication between them, her family starts to say bad things about Vijay. Vijay feels very bad about it. Aparna wants to tell Vijay the whole story, but she has no words after that. She does not know what to call the thing inside her. Sometimes it feels like an illness to her, sometimes a soul, sometimes the world's sorrow, and sometimes Jagatguru's wife's soul. Aparna feels like she made a mistake by coming to that house. What was inside her has grown, and the medication is affecting her body.

Vijay comes to Bhiwani to meet Aparna. Aparna's family members play the same blame game again. Vijay listens for a while. Everyone was sitting in the drawing room. Vijay also presents his arguments that it's not his fault. Your daughter behaves stubbornly.

Vijay tells Aparna's mother that Aparna is sick because of you people. You did not give her the right values. Everyone was talking among themselves. Aparna was listening for a long time. Aparna was also afraid that the inner voice might become louder again and Vijay might have to hear something from it.

Everyone was biased against each other to prove them wrong. And then suddenly they hear Aparna's voice... Oh, my dear husband. should I count myself in since the beginning of our marriage? Why does anyone get married? For happiness, right? The joy of becoming one from two. Do you even know the joy of becoming one from two? Did you think about the details you put on the matrimonial website before marriage? I have never seen a bigger liar than you. You showed me that you have a house. After marriage, it turned out to be your brother-in-law's. I had thought that after marriage, I would leave Delhi and shift to Raipur. But a month before the wedding, you sold your factory and said that you would start something new in Delhi. And you came to Delhi... completely empty. After marriage, I gave you all my savings and got your work started. That was the food stall. But even that did not work out. I was struggling in the field all day and listening to your failure story in the evening. My every month's salary and incentive were also invested in it. And today, you are telling me that I am sick. You gave me sickness, didn't you Vijay?

There was no financial support from your side, only expenses. I was alone, wandering around without any support, and even I was paying installments for your family's car. .... After marriage, our physical relationship was never right. Sometimes you would remember me in a month, sometimes in two. When I wanted to know the reason, I found out that you were busy watching porn and emptying yourself. When I asked you, you said you were sick... Since then, I have been suffering from your illness until today. It had been nine months since our marriage. I felt like I was standing alone and doing everything. During that time, you called your mother. From morning till evening, I have pushed around in the field, and when I came home tired in the evening, I had to take cooking classes from your mother. I became a good wife, but I was suffocating. That is why I left to work in Dubai. To breathe and understand what mistake I had made.

I had just started settling there when you fell ill. It had only been a month since I arrived. That night, you spoke to me in a muffled voice and asked me to come back. Without thinking, I booked a ticket and came back.

I helped you to get a job in the insurance industry, and I thought everything would be fine. However, nothing changed. After some time, I thought you were settled in your job. Maybe things would improve if I gave you some space. That is why when I got the option to transfer to Lucknow, I said yes. I had not been in Lucknow for 10 days, and you started showing your true colors again. You said goodnight to me and spent the whole night chatting with your female friend. Who is this female friend that you met on a matrimonial website? When I could not bear all these things, I made meditation my companion. I thought there was something wrong with me. I spent 10 days in a meditation center without a mobile phone and without contacting anyone. People say it is very difficult to stay in such a meditation center.

But should I tell you the truth, Vijay? I found it very easy to stay there ......The pain inside me gave me such fire that I focused all my energy on it....and I didn't find it difficult to stay there, ... neither asking anyone anything nor telling anyone anything.

No one was mine, nor was anyone else's. I did not have to express anything to anyone, and my life wasn't fake. I was just with myself there.... That is why being alone is ok for me.

I'm tired of trying to be a good wife and daughter-in-law in your family's race. I'm tired of trying to be a good daughter in your race. What is the point of such a family where I can't even express my own feelings and thoughts?... I'm a burden for my own family and just a tool for you. ...I don't want such fake relationships. If I must keep running in life, and there's no place to stop, then I prefer to run alone.

As Aparna continued to speak, she began to cry. After a while, she got up and walked to the roof.

She thought about it for a long time. Should she have said all of that? Sometimes it felt right, other times it felt like it was too much.

Vijay returned to Delhi without Aparna. All the belongings from their house in Paschim Vihar were brought to Bhiwani. Vijay had to shift to the PG (paying guest) accommodation because, without Aparna, he could not afford to pay the rent for their house.

Aparna had quit her job and was staying at home. She did not feel like staying at home, but there was no other place for her to go. If someone asked her something, she would answer. Most of the time she would sit lost in thought or in meditation.

Run Away Again

Aparna was talking to herself one day.

Aparna: Look, Mr. Ghost, where have you taken me? Now only you and I are left.

Voice: I did not take you anywhere. I just brought out what was inside you. So, if you keep carrying these feelings, you will exhaust yourself one day. Maybe at that time, you will not have the energy to run away again. So, it is better to take a break and see.

Aparna: Yes, Guruji, I have no choice but to listen to you. But this feels like jail to me. I want to get out of here. Life is not meant to be lived alone. I want to join a job again, somewhere. I want to talk to Vijay again.

Voice: You can do that anytime you want.

After such a long time, Aparna's phone rings. She sees that it is a call from an HR consultant, whom she may have spoken to many months ago. Aparna picks up the phone and talks to the consultant. He tells her that there is a vacant position for a branch manager in a Sodax Life Insurance Company for the Gurgaon location. Aparna suggests arranging an interview. The interview is arranged for the next day on Zoom. As soon as she hangs up the phone, Aparna gets lost in thought. She had just thought about leaving here, and now a job offer has come. It feels like a movie is playing, and she is just playing a role.

Voice: The job is done Finally

Aparna- Yes, there is some hope.

Aparna discusses this job offer with her family members and convinces them to let her go for the job if she got selected.

Three rounds of interviews have already been completed. Aparna is now silently praying to Lord Shiva for help in getting out of this situation.

After this, she assures her family members. She plans to go out on a trip. Summer has started. So, Aparna leaves for a solo trip to Bir Billing, Himachal. It is just her and her inner voice now. These days, she refers to that voice as her 'master'.

Aparna stays at a hostel on the first day, called Zoster Stay. There are lush green mountains all around the hostel. There is also a very large garden inside the hostel. Sitting alone so far away from home, after a few days, Aparna started to enjoy herself.

After checking in and having breakfast, around 11:00 am, Aparna went out for a walk.

As she was walking, she was talking to the master. Occasionally, some tourists were passing by. Sometimes they found a cherry tree and started eating cherries after picking them. Walking for almost half an hour, Aparna saw a Buddhist monastery on the way. She stopped and looked for a while, and then went inside. There she saw people distributing things like Prasad. But the Prasad they were distributing included pizza, cold drinks, biscuits, chips, etc. A lady gave Aparna some things as well. She wandered around the monastery for a while and then went towards the backyard. There, some stairs were descending, and there was a very big garden in front. The sunlight was coming straight from the front. Aparna went up the stairs and sat there.

Aparna said loudly, "Hey Master, all these people are eating here and they all seem so healthy and peaceful."

The voice replied, "It's not just about the food, Aparna. What is your perception of the food you are eating, what is your state of mind when you eat…That also matters. One day when you are in a good mood, you will easily digest spicy and heavy food. And on a bad day, even simple food like fruit and lentils will seem difficult to digest

Aparna: Yes, that is true. Anyway. I am feeling better today.

Voice: By the way, what are you thinking about for the future? What will you do next?

Aparna: I do not feel right talking to Vijay like this. I do not know why I was so harsh at that time. But there is another side to the coin. Think about it. What if I were a boy and he was a girl? Then what? The things I said to him that day, would not be able to hear myself saying them.

Many people try to start a new business but cannot succeed. After many failed businesses, I started a successful business. What I told him was wrong.

As for physical relationships, they are a biological need of the body. And understanding human's psychology is the most difficult job in this world.

I should not have talked to him in that way. It is my wedding anniversary after 2 days. I am going to Delhi to surprise Vijay.

By the way, Master. I still do not understand one thing. Who are you after all? Are you a ghost, just a creation of my mind, an angel, or are you really a guru? And what is your relationship with me?

Voice: understand it this way that I am just a wish of yours. You needed me. As for the relationship, you can consider me your friend. If you feel like having an extramarital affair, you can consider me your lover. And for now, I am also your guru. So, our relationship is that of a teacher and student. You have already given me the name, Master.

Aparna: hmm... well, I got it you will not tell me. Let's go, now let's wander a little more.

Aparna comes out of the monastery and starts walking with a waterfall outside. The path is rough. There are green trees and mountains all around.

Voice: All right, tell me one thing, do you believe in God? What is this rebirth, soul, and supreme being? According to you, what are these? Have you ever thought about how life goes on this earth? That there is life in trees and plants too.... also, in that butterfly. What do you know about that bird?

Aparna. Yes, I believe in God. I may not understand everything, but I want to understand. Since childhood, I have heard and believed in everything. Sometimes when I am alone, I think a lot, especially when I was silent for 10 days in a meditation center. Many thoughts came to my mind that never come to my mind normally. Sometimes it feels like I have seen the world through the glasses that the world has put on me, and I have never had my own experience. That is why I like to be alone sometimes, where nobody bores me with their stories. Whenever I talk to people, it is either they talk about themselves or they give me knowledge that I don't believe in the source. Today, most of my knowledge comes from TV, WhatsApp, and Facebook. I have no idea how much of it is true.

Voice: as much blood has been shed in the name of God in your world, it has not been shed for any other reason. And this happens because no human being has been able to reach its root. Everyone follows some customs of their ancestors and is satisfied with them. Then they want others to do the same. Those who have not experienced the soul or God themselves, do not have the right to say whether there is a soul or God. If there is God, then it is necessary to see Him, and if there is a soul, then it is also necessary to see it. Otherwise, believing in such things is a deception. In this sense, being an atheist is better.

You need to turn your mind inward, remove it from external things, centralize all your energy, and use it to examine your own mind so that you can understand your own nature. This is a very difficult task.

Therefore, when you were at home, I was watching you all the time to see if you were ready or not, but now it seems that you are ready. So, I would like to share something with you.

Aparna, "Yes. Anyway, you just told me that we have a guru-disciple relationship, so teach me what you want to teach. I am ready."

Voice, "I want to tell you that alongside the world you live in, there exists a parallel world called the astral world. Usually, you cannot see or hear it. But the people in that world can see you, hear you, touch you, and in fact, you cannot even imagine what they are doing with you."

Aparna, "What else can I expect from a ghost like you? Did you also come from the parallel world?"

Voice: I can understand that your IQ is very low to understand all this.

Aparna: Does that mean you are insulting me?

Voice: No, I am just trying to explain it to you.

Let me make it easy for you. I will explain it in your language. Do you know that human ears can only hear from 20 hertz to 20,000 hertz? And human eyes can only react to wavelengths ranging from 380 nanometers to 750 nanometers.

If you search for this information on Google, you will find it in your world too. But, all of this depends on the brain's capacity

The eye transmits information to the brain but some characteristics of the signal are lost and altered during the process. If you search, you will find that there is evidence in your world as well that using the right amount of electric current to change human brainwaves can increase human brain capacity. Many developed countries are conducting research in this field. Neuroscience is also very advanced in your world. However, the r world that I am talking about, is much more advanced than you and is ahead of you in time. You, humans, do not even fully understand the concept of time and space.

Can you tell me if we are the only living beings in this entire universe on this earth? Is there no life anywhere else in the entire universe? Will time travel ever be possible even after 100 years from now? Do you have any idea about the research that has been done on the human brain so far?

In one human brain, there are approximately 14 to 16 billion neurons in the cerebral cortex and 55 to 70 billion neurons in the cerebellum. These are all neurons. Synapses connect with each other through these neurons. The technique to solidify these connections is already available.

Aparna: if all this is true, then you are telling me that I cannot see or feel that another world. And even if there is such a world, someone must have discovered it or known about it in that parallel world, right?

Voice: To locate even their one place, many people were killed. Their lab centers were far outside your frequency range. Let me tell you about the location of a center from some time ago. The Bermuda Triangle is a lab in the Atlantic Ocean, covering an area of 300,000 square kilometers. It is known for the mysterious disappearance of more than 50 ships and 20 airplanes. The area is shaped like a triangle, stretching from Florida, Panhandle, Bermuda, and Greater Antilles. Columbus wrote about it in his book, and in 1964, Vincent Gaddis named it the Devil's Triangle. Ships suddenly sink here, and engines shut down. Even if someone wanted to swim, they could not. In 1942, American navy ships passing through lost contact and were destroyed. Rescue teams sent after them also disappeared. Bruce Gernot sailed there in 1970 and returned safely, but experienced strange phenomena. The ship's electronic gadgets turned off, and it sped up to 3,000 kilometers per hour, covering 150 kilometers in 3 minutes. The Bermuda Triangle remains a mystery

Aparna crossed checked the information on the internet she found he was right about that Bermuda story.

Aparna, what are you all talking about? Then how is he still alive? Voice, those scientists who live in the lab there can control the entire frequency around them. When ships are built in your world, they are made according to the density of the ocean. Whenever a ship approached their lab, they would reduce the density of the water, causing the ship to sink. The techniques they use are still not available to you. And maybe in the next 50 years, they will not be available either. That world will always be ahead of you.

When Bruce German became a pilot in 1970 and was able to take his ship out of there, it was a lesson for those scientists too. For the first time, they realized that human willpower is also a very high energy. As long as you don't accept death, no one can kill you.

Aparna: now the story does not make sense to me throughout the whole film. Earlier you were saying that the world is much more advanced than us and we do not know what they are doing with us, and now you are saying that we are more powerful than them with our willpower, assets, etc. What are you talking about?

Voice: Well, do you remember when you had bhang in Mathura that day, and you saw a road along with this road? There you saw an accident. Try to remember that accident

Aparna, I am getting some faint memories. Aparna recalls that memory and closes her eyes while thinking. Suddenly, as if a 3D video starts playing in front of her closed eyes. She sees that the accident was not someone else's, but hers. As soon as she sees herself in that accident, her eyes suddenly open.

Voice: What was that? Did you understand anything? That was you. In that place, in one possibility, you had died.

You did not accept death unconsciously and immediately entered another possibility.

Aparna: does it mean that I am some kind of God that I am dying in one possibility in one word and then talking about what is next in another?

Voice: you are special and many people are watching you, whom you cannot see. In fact, many people are learning from you. You are free will.

This is your uniqueness. The earth is not as ordinary as it seems. There are many parallel worlds here, and many concepts that you have never seen or heard of before. There is no coincidence in your world, nothing at all. For example, your name is Aparna. This is not a coincidence. Why is your city of Bhiwani called a small Kashi? Why is your neighborhood called Bharat Nagar?

The meaning of all these things is that you will gradually understand them. As you get closer to nature, nature will slowly reveal all its secrets to you. And you have the ability to understand all those things that are very important for you to know.

Aparna, well, I am not really understanding anything special. But as you are saying, Master. You said that someone is always watching me. Is this 24/7 surveillance just for me or does everyone see it?

Voice: Everyone is on observation, and not just observation, some people are completely puppets. The thinking of many humans is not even their own. Anyway, in your world, there are multiple things that can affect thinking. Then the rest of the people in the parallel world complete the gaps.

In this world of yours, every living being's eyes are like cameras for those people. All electronic devices are in their control. Your time, activity, and thoughts can all be controlled by them. There are very few people who are truly free in this world. This free will is real wealth.

Your world's people are busy fighting each other. You must have seen it too. Many times, on TV, people of different groups and religions argue and debate with each other. If asked where their information comes from, it will be clear that the source of more than half of their information is wrong. Their information comes from WhatsApp, Facebook, YouTube videos, and people who consider themselves intelligent. That is all there is to the source of that information.

When it comes to history, do you humans fight among yourselves, does anyone have any proof that history was the same as written, taught, or told to you? You try to convince each other of things. Do you humans have any proof to believe in that yourselves?

Your own five senses are controlled by the people of parallel worlds.

There are similar groups there as well. Some organizations only observe you guys. But just like in your world, there are also negative forces in parallel worlds that want to control everything. Before you went to your Upasana center, you were also one of them. As you become more conscious, you were becoming more free-willed.

I am just starting to feel it now. It is very difficult to believe in all these things. But trust me. I will gradually feel and show you everything.

Aparna: what do you mean I will show you?

Voice: You'll have to train yourself to be like that. Right now, you are stable.

Come on, I will show you a trailer. Just keep following me. If you stay with me, I can show you.

Aparna: anyway, there are not many special options. Just show me what you want to show and get done what you want to get done. Just don't make me jump off a mountain." "What do you want me to do?" "

Voice: go to the market area where there are some people. As Aparna walks, she arrives at the main market of Bir Billing.

There is a pedestal in front of an ATM of a state bank where people and shops in the surrounding area are clearly visible. Following the voice, she sits on a three-seater iron chair there.

Aparna: "I have arrived at the location, show me what to see?"

Voice: Just follow the method of concentration you have learned in meditation. Follow the concentration as I guide you. Close your eyes, take a deep breath, and slowly release it. Focus on your breathing for a while. Slowly bring your attention to your face. Focus on all your body parts, from head to toe. Listen to all the sounds inside and outside

Approximately 10 minutes later... Aparna feels that her entire body has become very sensitive. She can hear all the noise inside and outside very clearly. Her breathing has become slow. Her heartbeat has become very slow. She can feel all the sensations of her body. She can feel the air on the outer layer of her body.

Voice, concentrate all your energy in one place. Just like all sensations are coming on one side. Feel all the sensations on your face. Feel as if all the energy of your entire body is being focused in one place.

(Aparna follows the voice.)

Now feel all your energy in your eyes.

(After a while)

Now slowly open your eyes.

Aparna opens her eyes and looks around.

Aparna: What is this? What is this? I can really see it.

Aparna sees that above every person's head, there is an inverted image of a person hanging, like a painting made of colorful currents. It was like the lightning she had seen in the sky, in which a colored image of a person was inserted. Some people also had a straight white line above them. This line was just like the one she had seen above the crematorium while traveling from Delhi to Bhiwani. All the images above the people were different from each other. This lasted for a few moments and then everything returned to normal. She could see it for about 30 to 40 seconds. Now Aparna had a lot of questions in her mind.

The voice said, "Yes, you are thinking right. The people with a straight white line above their heads are not connected or partially connected. And those whose pictures you saw, a clone has been made from their energy bodies. They are fully connected and controlled."

"Did you notice one thing? Most of the locals living here are the ones who have free will."

Suddenly, Aparna feels a tremble in her body and a dryness in her throat.

Aparna: I am feeling a bit strange.

Voice: Yes, that was bound to happen. That is enough for today. Have a mixed fruit juice around here and go back to the hotel. We can discuss the rest of the matters there.

Aparna takes a deep breath and leaves the place while speaking to herself.

Aparna: Oh Lord Shiva, what is going on here? I cannot understand anything. Please save me.

Shiva Shambho. Shiva Shambho. Shiva Shambho.

Aparna wanders around the market for a while, drinks juice, and tries some local dishes. Then she heads back to the hotel.

By the time she reaches the hotel, it is already evening.

She goes to the hotel and sees people sitting in the garden. Old people are sitting there, some are reading Nobel. Some are sitting together, having tea and snacks.

Aparna: Are you watching, Master? How comfortably people are sitting? They are eating and drinking. And you scare me every day. Everything is normal here."

Voice: The good thing is that most people in your world are still normal. But you do not know that 50 years ago people enjoyed more than this. Your world is in a semi-machine age. Not everyone in every place is normal. Relax a bit now, we will talk in the evening. By the way, it's time for your evening tea.

Aparna walks towards the canteen and orders tea. Then she comes back and sits at a table. Aparna was also a little confused from the inside. But she also realized that she did not feel lonely anymore because of being with her master.

Aparna was looking at the people around her. The tea had arrived. She had just taken a sip when a woman of about 35 years old came and sat at her table. She started talking to Aparna and told her that she gives healing sessions to people and conducts meditation. Aparna talked to her for a while. While talking, she told Aparna that there is an ancient temple of Kali Mata nearby and she should go there.

She gives Aparna the number of a local cab driver there. Aparna calls the cab driver right in front of that woman and plans to visit Kali Mata temple the next morning.

After a while, the woman leaves, and Aparna sits there for a while. She overhears people talking and learns that dinner orders must be placed in advance. So, Aparna gets up and goes to the hotel's in-house restaurant to place her dinner order. After placing the order, she goes back to her room.

At this time, Aparna felt a slight connection from within. She felt more connected than her inner voice. As if she had found a new friend.

She knew that Meditation is something that opens up new layers of understanding for humans. But her experience was her own. She had never heard of it before. Yet now, she was gradually becoming more comfortable with the voice inside her.

She also remembered Vijay. The conversations with her family members also came to mind. She was planning to go to Delhi in three days

Then the voice inside her. Voice: You are beyond my understanding. After understanding and seeing everything, why do you want to go back to Vijay? Aparna: I do not know. Maybe when we are in a situation, we cannot see it that way. We can only see it from a distance outside the situation. I got married, so I should fulfill my responsibilities, right? And by the way, are you feeling jealous? Oh my God, I had forgotten. You are also my lover. So, when are you going to tell me who you are?

In fact, you did not even help me figure out who I am. Apart from that, you are telling me everything.

Now talking to you does not feel weird anymore. It seems like a part of my daily routine. Strange, isn't it? Master: Well, let me tell you one thing. When I eat and drink, can you also feel those things? Dialogue, smell, all of that?

Voice: Sometimes I am there, sometimes I'm not.

Aparna: How do you look, good?

Voice: Just like you. Nowadays, I only see what's there.

Aparna: You don't even show your own face to your friends? You don't say anything and just keep talking nonsense. You give useless knowledge, don't you?

Aparna: All right, tell me about that world. How does it look?

Voice: It's a magical world. Recently, those people discovered that your world and that world are connected to each other.

You can see it in this way, when the present consciousness energy is here, the same consciousness is not present there. If I'm correct, it's a game of conscious and unconscious energy.

In the beginning, they thought that you were just puppets for them. Slowly things started to make sense.

When people become unconscious here, the people in that world can use your body as they wish. Until a few years ago, they used your dreams and nights, you have no idea

Now there are some surveillance agencies there. There are some new protocols. Things are better than before. Even now, some organizations are using this human body here in illegal ways.

You may have noticed that usually at night when you sleep and wake up the next day, there is more fatigue in your body than rest. Most people here have been cloned from energy bodies. They are machines that look exactly like humans. The backbone of artificial intelligence has ruined everything there. Your leaders, film stars, and businessmen, all have their clones there. The videos they make and send on your internet. They use your five senses through your body to experience it

Money is everything at your place, and in that world, the profound experience of the five senses is everything. They send direct, multiply-time messages to your body and fully control your body and thoughts. Then you do what they want you to do. Controlling people in a place with advanced technology is as easy as that place's technology is advanced. Places with high populations are on their target hit list.

For example, if you currently live in Delhi, you may have noticed that time slows down when you are in your city Bhiwani, but as soon as you go to Delhi, time seems to fly there.

There, people watch you 24/7. Then they target some people among you and use them for experimentation. First, they come to you through mobile TV and bring changes in your thinking. When your thoughts start flowing in the same direction, they pass the desired message through your brainwaves. Artificially, they nurture a desire within you, and then targeted people to do the same things that they want. This has been happening for many years.

Aparna: when so much control is in the hands of the people of a world, it is impossible to avoid them. And to be honest, Master, all this seems like nonsense to me, considering everything that has been happening in these past few days. Whether you are a ghost or my illness, I have accepted both. I am not understanding what you are saying. If everything was so upside down in the world, then how is the world still functioning? According to me, my world is perfect, and despite all the flaws, everyone is still moving forward. Neither life nor anything else is affected. Now, if you want to explain something, keep explaining. If I understand, then great, if not, that's okay too. What difference does it make?

Voice: You know, you are so fearless and careless, and that is also your quality and your weakness. Anyway, now our relationship is that of a teacher and student, and I must tell you that even after having so much control, the world is still functioning because people still have their conscious energy. Well, just tell me one thing - do you want to understand what a human being truly is and what God is?

Aparna: even if I say no, you will still make me understand, right?

Aparna gets up and walks towards the balcony. There is a house with a courtyard in front of her, and a cherry tree is growing in it. Aparna was looking at that house and the tree quietly.

Voice: Look at this tree, see how life is happening in it. Leave aside its spiritual aspect, and look at its scientific aspect. Everything you see in the world is created from the earth. This tree grew from the earth. Its branches, leaves, cherries, everything is a gift of nature. There is life in every particle of this tree. Air, sunlight, water, and earth have all played their part in this.

These trees and plants do not speak in a language that we can hear. We do not even feel that they are communicating with each other. Yet, they all communicate with each other. They are more connected to nature than we are.

A jungle has its own ecosystem which is complete in itself. For a plant to feed itself, everything it needs is automatically provided by nature. Similarly, when humans stay connected to nature, they will receive all the necessary nutrients. In this air, everything that you need is present. However, most of the time, humans rely on guidance from the environment around them rather than listening to their own bodies. That is why they cannot connect with nature.

There are many yogis in your world who have proven that the human body functions not just by eating but also by being connected to nature. There was an experiment that was conducted here with a yogi named Prahalad Jani who was kept in a hospital for 10 days without eating or drinking anything.

There is also a person in Goa from the USA named Elite Olm-Men who is a breatharian and is alive without eating.

Aparna: why are you telling me all this? What difference does it make to me? Are you saying that I should stop eating now?

Voice: No. I am not saying that you should stop eating, but you can reduce the amount of food you eat at the beginning. This will help you in your future training. If most of your body's energy is spent digesting food, you won't be able to learn. In fact, the human body doesn't need so much food. There are many other tools to keep the body's energy levels up, which you have no idea about. You get energy from the sun, air, water, and nature. You just have to train your body in that way.

From today, reduce the amount of food you eat and make some changes in your diet. Because the journey ahead is not easy.

Aparna: it feels like I've enlisted in the army and I'm about to go to war. Anyway, there's no turning back now. All right, let us start today.

Voice: Well then, let us wait for what? Let us have dinner and take a little walk to aid digestion.

Aparna goes downstairs to have food. After having food, she takes a walk and talks to her master.

Aparna, okay master tells me this. If I want to stop your chatter at any time, what should I do?

Voice: It's very simple. I am connected to your body, so I will always be listening to you. But if you want me to immediately stop, you need to put your tongue on the roof of your mouth and I will be quiet.

Aparna: All right, that's also a mechanism. Anyway, it was important to know this.

By the way, you know everything about me. But I still don't know anything about you. And you will not tell me. Anyways…. When you were talking about the other world, does that mean they relate to us 24/7? Sometimes there are breaks too.

Voice: You can think of it as controlling or observing a human body from this world. When consciousness is present in a particular body, the body connected to that one becomes unconscious, and when the body here is unconscious, the body there becomes conscious. When the body here is unconscious, at that time, they can control that unconscious body through the conscious body. After gaining control, they research and test it in various ways. Many times, they use the clone of this body from your world to use its feelings, emotions, and experiences according to their own will.

Aparna, you said that our world is a semi-machine age. And the parallel world is more advanced in technology, so is that world a machine age?

Voice: Yes. That world is a machine age. It is a machine that looks like a human. Children are not born in their mother's wombs but in machines. After that, any human machine is given a memory chip.

They do open business.... Anything can be modified in the body according to one's own will. Rich people never die. It's a magical world. Aparna, do people there believe in God? Voice, believing in God is not a thing. They know that there is a conscious energy that drives every conscious being.

Aparna: can I see all this? Can I go there or somehow see it?

Voice: yes, but you'll need training for that. That's why I'm preparing you. If you learn to transfer your conscious energy, it's possible.

"Resume your meditation practice again. You just need to remember the things that you already know. You just forgot a little bit.

Aparna: I never know when you might have to defuse a bomb. But restarting your meditation practice is not a big deal. I can do that.

Voice: practice being alert first. Your meditation should be 24/7, whether you are awake, sleeping, eating, or drinking, you need to be conscious of every activity. As you're walking now, you should feel your footsteps on the ground. Be conscious of this. When you breathe in, feel the air going all the way inside. Learn to feel the air that enters your body. What I am teaching you cannot be achieved in just one day. Meditation cannot be done by simply closing your eyes and sitting.

Aparna: Yes, I understand what you are trying to say. Okay, I will start right away. By the way, how much time will it take approximately?

Voice: It might take around six months or a little more than that. Whatever I am teaching you, the amazing thing is that I learned it from you only.

Aparna: Learned from me?

Voice: When I connected with you, I received a lot of information in your unconscious memory. I am also learning with you. Your memory and activity have been used by an artificial intelligence agency for a long time in another world. You will gradually learn a lot of things. For now, make yourself as sensitive as possible. Be alert to your every action, reaction, feeling, and emotion.

Aparna starts practicing staying alert that day. She learns conscious sleep that night.

The next day, as per the plan, the driver comes to pick up Aparna, and she sets off for Kali Mata Temple. With her face out of the car window, feeling the breeze and looking at the lush green valleys around, she reaches the Kali Mata Temple. The temple environment was very calm. The temple was completely empty, except for a priest sitting there. Aparna wanders in different parts of the temple. After roaming for a while, she sits in front of the idol of Kali Mata in meditation.

Voice: "Do you know the meaning of Kali Mata and why she is worshipped? Why did your ancestors worship her?

Aparna: "Why do you waste time asking questions? Just tell me what you want to say, Master."

Voice: "Kali Mata is the goddess of time, in which all good and bad things happen. Everything good and bad happens in time. The meaning of Kali is that which is unlimited.

Your ancestors worshipped the old form of Kali Mata, whose form has completely changed now.

when time is seen as feminine energy, it is Kali. When it is seen as masculine energy, it is Mahakal or Shiva.

Time creates and destroys everything. Whatever is happening here is within time, and the reason for that event is hidden within time. This is what creates the universe."

If you understand Kali, you will understand the multiverse. If you know Kali, you will know the time. Then you will understand parallel words.

Aparna: What are you trying to create by relating all these things? What kind of stew are you trying to feed me?

Voice: You are currently in this Possible World here your understanding is limited in it. To understand all of this, you will have to drop your logical mind. That is why your ancestors have told you many stories. These temples, prayers, and rituals? Through all of these, they have told you something. You will understand it slowly.

For now, just focus and gather positive energy here. Aparna brings her attention back to her breaths and starts meditating again. After a while, she gets up, goes to the priest, and gives him a donation of ₹500 in the worship plate. She takes the prasad and returns.

The voice asks, "Why did you leave the money here?"

Aparna replies, "This temple is so unique. Very few people visit here. The priest here is living alone with his family. So, I thought maybe I could help. They are maintaining it with so much cleanliness. I felt good going there."

The voice says, "Yes, I already knew about it. But I am aware of your activity and alerting you."

Aparna replies, "Yes, Master, I understand."

Aparna sits near a waterfall next to the temple. She watches the flowing water, the butterflies flying around, and the birds chirping and feeling everything around her. Aparna was observing all of this, feeling everything, and had a smile on her face.

Aparna emptied her water bottle and refilled it with the water from the waterfall. She drank some and started walking towards her cab. The driver was waiting there. Aparna asked the driver about the places to visit nearby.

Just then, a voice interrupted them, "Won't you go to that Shiva temple? Go to that Shiva temple."

There is a very old Shiva temple in Himachal Pradesh. The Baidya Nath Shiv Temple is an important place for people who come from far and wide for their religious faith. This temple attracts many devotees, foreign tourists, and pilgrims from all over India throughout the year. Aparna leaves for the temple in the same cab.

Aparna: you also know that I have been to this temple before,"

she spoke. "I mean, everything that is in my memory. You know all of that, right, Master?"

The voice said, "No, I don't know everything. But yes, I know most things."

While talking to Master, Aparna reaches the temple. Aparna also meditates even while sitting in that temple. She also feels that her body is more sensitive after leaving the temple. And focusing here in the temple was quite different. She has been to this place before. But this time it feels like she has taken something from this temple with her body.

As the day passes, Aparna returns to the hotel.

Aparna: I think I should talk to Vijay today. In fact, I should prepare to meet him.

Voice: Yes, you should do it if it feels right.

Aparna calls Vijay and during the conversation, she also asks for his current address.

After talking to Vijay, Aparna feels better than before.

Aparna regretted her actions but she knew that nobody could understand her situation. So, she found a middle ground in her mind.

Aparna continued with the practice recommended by her master. Now, she decides to stay more active and gradually increase her consciousness.

Trying To Settle Again

The next day, Aparna books a bus to Delhi from Beer Billing. During the day, she buys a bottle of local fruit wine from the local market. The bus drops her off at Majnu ka Tilla Road in the morning, from where she takes a cab to Vijay's place. Aparna arrives at Vijay's room, knocking on the gate with a bottle of fruit wine and a flower bouquet.

Seeing Aparna there, Vijay forgets everything and they spend time together. Aparna tells Vijay about her new job offer. After spending the whole day together, everything becomes normal again. Now they were a happy couple once again.

Aparna is maintaining her routine of practicing meditation and striving to remain conscious. Now, it has become a habit for her to engage in conversations with her Master, and she learns something new from these conversations every day. Aparna is making progress in her spiritual journey and is continuously seeking to expand her understanding.

Aparna and Vijay have shifted to Gurugram. she has adjusted to a new environment and continues to progress in her journey toward consciousness.

Aparna has joined her new office. Her routine remains the same, with sales meetings, office conference calls, and evening tea with Vijay. The only thing that has changed was Aparna herself. She was not the same inside anymore. From the outside, she looked completely normal, but inside her, the training was ongoing. Every day, she experienced something new, which sometimes felt like magic.

The Master was helping Aparna understand that this creation is the most magnificent creation of God. This is a divine play whose secret has not been fully understood by great sages, monks, and modern scientists who have made a lot of effort to understand it.

There are many supernatural forces in this world that affect us. The Sun, Moon, and planets all have an impact on us. The movements of the Sun, Moon, Saturn, Mars, and other planets influence our future and affect us. The Sun's spots and the 11-year cycle of the fire that occurs on the Sun affect the structure of human blood. Aparna is having new experiences these days. She listens to the Master's advice and tries out different colored clothes to wear during her period cramps. Aparna is feeling new changes in her body every day. Her body is becoming more sensitive than before. Her focus is clearer than before.

Even without any specific diet, her weight is decreasing. Now she is feeling more sensitive toward people's feelings than before. Now, while walking through the crowd, she can see colorful lights like some current above people's heads. Because of those lights above the people around her, she can see changes in their behavior, facial expressions, and body language.

Gradually, Aparna is gaining confidence in her inner voice. In about three months, her body had reached a position where she could not distinguish between sleep, dream, and wakefulness. She was very sensitive in every condition. Master was teaching Aparna to consciously dream and control them.

Aparna had now reached a state where she was not only training during the day but also at night. Aparna's and Vijay's relationship had once again reached a point where they were just roommates.

Aparna also noticed that Vijay was not particularly affected by this fact. He was not very bothered about Aparna.

One day, Master told Aparna that she would have to stay alone for a few days. Aparna was wondering how it would be possible to stay alone again and again. And that same evening, Vijay announced that he was taking a 15-day vacation to his hometown.

Aparna found it very strange at first. It felt like the whole universe was there to teach her something.

Opening The New Dimension

On June 3, 2022, Vijay leaves. Upon Master's suggestion, Aparna quickly comes home from the office that day.

Voice: You have a very strong mind, that is why whenever you get tense, you create a walking energy field within yourself. Now you must take a step forward today.

"Whatever you say, my lord," Aparna replied.

Voice: "Feel yourself. You are a conscious energy. You are in this body. Your body is actually in your mind."

Aparna follows the direction.

Voice: "What is your existence? Feel it. When I speak, 'I,' what is this 'I'? This body is not just me; everything is you. Slowly, feel it inside this body.

Inside and outside of this body, it is you. Feel this room. It is you. This is the creation of your mind. Expand your attention."

Relate everything to yourself....

You are in the house, feel the entire building.

Listen carefully to all the sounds around you, from the heartbeat inside your body to the noises outside. Slowly spread your focus. Feel the whole city. Extend yourself beyond the city and feel all the surrounding cities. Feel yourself in the middle of a big circle where you can take your attention to wherever you want.

That everything is you. All these people, all these living beings, everything is you.

Aparna is feeling her body as if it is at the center of all these things as if a current is flowing through her body. Slowly, she does not feel her own body. Slowly, she realized that she does not feel the boundaries of her body. There is just noise, just a sound.

Now, she is just listening to that sound. Sometimes the twitching nerves, and the sound of vehicle horns due to the road, she can filter each sound and hear it. But now, she cannot feel the distance of any noise. She doesn't know where the noise is coming from. She doesn't know which thing is inside, or which is outside.

Following the sound, Aparna opens her eyes. Nearly four hours passed, but Aparna only felt it for 5-7 minutes.

"What was that, Master? How did so much time pass? Why didn't I realize?" Aparna asks.

Voice: as soon as you detach yourself from this body, you lose track of time.

Aparna: after today's experience, I have even more questions in my mind. What is my true existence? Who am I? No matter how many spiritual books I have read, and no matter which religious gurus we listen to, they all say that I am not this body. Today, I felt that I did not even feel my body, yet I was still there. What is all this?

Voice: see, if you have ever seen a mental person, in your eyes, he will appear to be doing very strange actions. But in his mind, he has his own complete world. He is feeling this world, living in it, and to us, he appears crazy. It is possible that the world that is shown to you, is shown differently to others. He sees, smells, and talks just like you do, but not in this dimension, in another dimension that is not within your reach.

Now, you have no evidence that you are not crazy. In reality, no one has it. Whatever world you see, and feel, is a creation of your own mind.

I have told you before. We are all part of a big brain. Whenever you want, you can change the state of your mind and change the entire environment around you. But it is not that easy. You can build as much body as you want. You can enter a completely new world through your mind, but every action has a reaction. If you want, I can show you because you are completely ready now.... You said you want to see me.

Aparna: I have gone through so much madness that now I am not afraid like before. To tell you the truth, this subject of meditation is so vast that even if I devote my entire life to it, it will not be enough. Do you think I am ready? Then let us do whatever experiment is left.

Voice: Okay then let us do the experiment tonight. But for that, you will also have to use emotions, without any questions. Like actors do in movies. Someone becomes someone's husband, someone becomes someone's boyfriend, someone becomes someone's wife, and someone becomes someone's girlfriend. So, you will have to use your emotions and imagination too.

Aparna, yes, I will do it.

Upon Master's request, Aparna calls all the household members in the evening and tells them that she is not feeling well and will be going to bed early tonight. Vijay had already reached his home, and Aparna had informed the household members through phone calls. Dinner was not allowed that day. Aparna takes a bath at night, wears comfortable clothes, and goes to bed as per the Master's instructions.

Voice: just like we did before, spread your attention and go up to the sky this time. And neutralize yourself.

Aparna returns to the same condition where there is no body, only sound.

Voice: now slowly shift all your five senses into an imagination. First, we will transfer touch. As I speak, feel yourself more and more. ...Where I am taking you is where you have been before. You already know that place.

You are in a 16*16 size room with white paint. You are lying on a white king-size bed. Feel your body lying down. Your skin is touching the bed. You are lying straight. There is a pillow under your head. You have covered yourself with a thin soft blanket up to your chest. There is very dim light in the room. There is a window behind the headboard of the bed.

Feel yourself in this room. You are here. Now slowly feel your breath. As your breath becomes slow, you are in deep sleep. You are sleeping. Keep feeling yourself and sleep.

Aparna falls asleep in deep slumber for a while. She opens her eyes and looks around in shock. She is indeed somewhere else. It is a very large luxurious master bedroom. The room is just as the master had described it. She looks at her hands, touches her face, and everything feels like magic to her. She is feeling completely different waves in her body. She had never felt this kind of vibration before.

She speaks in a scared, trembling voice, "Master, where are you? Where am I?"

No sound can be heard.

She felt like her body was vibrating like a drug. The vibrations were making her body feel very pleasurable. Her eyes could see 50% clearer than before. Her sense of smell had increased. She could feel the light perfume scent in the room clearly. She looked around the room from all sides. She moved the curtain from the window behind the bed. She was really in a magical world. She felt like she was in a palace.

This was a strange feeling, with a little bit of fear, a little bit of happiness, and a little bit of excitement.

The New World

When Aparna opened the gate to go outside, she saw a boy coming towards her. He was about 33 years old, approximately 5.8 feet tall, and had a dusky complexion. His face somewhat resembled a sage, and he looked ruggedly handsome. He was wearing a white shirt and blue jeans and was clean-shaven. His eyes had a unique sparkle.

Aparna was just looking at him as he approached from the front when he suddenly hugged her tightly and cried out, "I knew you would do it. I know you're confused right now, but let me explain it to you." Aparna was just seeing and feeling all of this and listening to him. She felt his familiar perfume scent. His touch felt very good as if he had a special connection with her as if all her fears had disappeared when he hugged her. Aparna just stood there, feeling everything. He put both his hands on Aparna's face and with tears in his eyes, he said, "I'm Vasu. Your husband," and with that, he kissed her forehead.

Aparna: "Vasu??? You... you are the master?... What... I just came from somewhere else, what?" As Aparna speaks, he touches her hands and feet, her entire body. The same pleasurable vibration is felt as if it were an intoxication.

Aparna wants to move that boy away from her. But the experience of his touch is unlike any other. She doesn't understand anything, yet this feeling is pleasurable for her.

Vasu: Yes, I am your master. I'm sorry, but I didn't have any other way. I can't imagine my life without you.

Aparna was feeling as if Vasu was talking to her from very close. The scent of his breath, his touch, his eyes, everything was not in her memory, yet he felt very familiar.

Aparna: I am starting to understand a little. So, you have been training me for so many days to bring me here. You could have told me all this earlier. Now, I am feeling crazier than ever. Is it true or false? I do not know anything....

Is this another planet? .... What place is this? And what is happening to my body?

This is strange. As she was speaking, Aparna's legs were shaking.

Vasu: I will tell you everything. First, you need to stabilize yourself as you are currently in a high-vibration state. You have just entered this body.

Saying this, Vasu lifts Aparna in his arms and places her back on the bed. He pours water into a glass from a jug on a side table and gives it to Aparna.

Aparna drinks the water, but as soon as she finishes, she feels even more thirsty. In a short while, she drinks the entire jug of water.

Aparna: I don't know what it. this is my dream or what...but it feels real. Whatever it is, it's very beautiful. I have never stayed in such a beautiful bedroom before. ...

And you, Mr. Vasu, stay a little away from me. Just because you say so, you are not my husband. First, explain the whole story to me, because I cannot handle two husbands in the same memory. I was trying to meditate and you made me crazy and insane.

Vasu is just smiling at Aparna and tears are streaming down her eyes.

Aparna: oh man… you are strange.

Why are you crying? Crying and being afraid are what I should be doing right now. But it is amazing that the vibrations in my body are such that I can't even cry. And I am not even scared...

Vasu shakes his head as he looks at Aparna. Sitting next to her, he takes her hand and says, "You're still on earth, it's a different dimension. It exists parallel to the earth. We're in a lab right now."

Aparna: So, am I dead? I have left my body.

Vasu: No, you are alive and you have left your time and space. We also call this place Alfa Earth. This place is a little ahead of the time and space where you stay. That is why our technology is more advanced. One minute there is equal to an hour here. So, one day has passed here in 24 minutes in your time there. Your body is in rest mode. You will stay here for about 21 days. When you go back there, only one night will have passed.

Here, your body had died. I had become very lonely. I wanted to see you conscious in some way, so I too left my body. That is why we had to stay in the lab here.

Aparna: for me, …. this thing is like magic. …I do not understand anything special.

And I have come so far ahead that it is not possible to go back from here.

(While talking, she was looking around the room, watching herself. She was looking at Vasu and sometimes look outside through the window.)

After a few seconds of silence, she said" This place is amazing, buddy. …. I need to go to the bathroom.

Vasu points towards the gate on the left side of the room and says, "Yes, this way. Your body will stabilize in a few moments. Come on, I'll take you there." Aparna replies, "No, I'm already stable enough. I'll be back in a minute from the bathroom." Aparna goes towards the bathroom, opens the gate, and looks around thinking, "This bathroom is as big as my bedroom, or maybe even bigger."

Aparna had never thought that a bathroom could be so luxurious and magnificent. She was both confused and excited. She looked at herself in the mirror hanging in the bathroom. Aparna saw that she was wearing a soft grey nightie. Her face was lighter than before, and her skin was glowing and smooth. Her hair was long, dark, and thick. Her body was in the best possible shape. She felt very different in this body. Everything seemed like a dream. Everything felt so strange, but she still wanted to stay in it. After spending a long time looking at herself in the bathroom, Aparna returned to the room. Vasu was sitting and tapping his foot, waiting for Aparna to come back.

Aparna understood all the gestures in his eyes. His gaze was such that every girl wants her partner to look at her with such eyes. There was love, possessiveness, and thirst in those eyes. Aparna looked towards Vasu and then lowered her gaze and sat on the bed.

Aparna: Master, can you please stop looking at me like that? Look, this is very new to me and it also feels very strange. Please, can you explain to me exactly where we are and what is happening?

Vasu: Aparna, it will take you some time to understand all of this.

This is just another possibility of life on Earth. Everything here is almost the same as on Earth. The names of all countries are almost the same. The names of all places are almost the same. People are also almost the same. Life appears the same when seen. But still, there is another parallel space in different terms of meaning.

If I tried to explain all of this to you there, you would not understand. Now that you are here, you will experience it all. You will understand everything through your experience.

You are here for the first time. We have plenty of time. Your body will adjust to the frequency here. Let us first go home.

Aparna, Home? Yes. Okay.

Aparna was still feeling a slight buzz. There were many questions in her mind, but what should she ask first? And later, she could not understand anything.

Vasu puts a hand on Aparna's shoulder and looks into her eyes, then says, "Don't worry, everything is okay. I'm with you." Vasu takes Aparna's hand and leads her outside the room. Aparna keeps following him. They come out into the hallway from the gallery.

Aparna sees that there are many people there. There is a reception from where they are leaving. Everyone is bowing their head slightly towards Vasu and greeting him with a good morning as well as towards Aparna. They come out of the building and there is a black car standing outside the entrance gate. Seeing the view outside, Aparna's eyes widen in surprise.

Aparna is watching everything in amazement. Vasu opens the front gate of the car and signals her to sit, while he sits on the driver's seat from the other side. Vasu keeps looking at Aparna intermittently as they drive.

Aparna is looking at the magical place. It is morning time and the sun is shining lightly. The roads are very clean and tidy. There is greenery all around, and birds of different kinds are perched on the trees. Fresh air is blowing.

She looks inside the car. The car is fully automatic from the inside. She had never seen such luxury cars before. She looks towards Vasu and asks, "Which city is this? What do they call it here?"

Vasu says, "This is Delhi, and we are in India."

Aparna says, "But I know Delhi very well, and it is completely different. How is this place built, how is this possible?"

Vasu says, "Now, what should I tell you? When we go back to the lab, I will show you. This world is a strange illusion."

"For now, let's just go and we reach home. Take your time to digest everything."

"Come on, I'll play some good music for you.

A light melody begins. This music soothes Aparna a lot. She has heard it before. Aparna is looking, the city is completely clean. Houses, streets, intersections, markets, and everywhere. It is clean. No dust, dirt, or traffic jams can be seen anywhere.

Vasu is telling Aparna about the city as they walk along the way. Vasu explains that green spaces have been left everywhere in this city. He keeps describing the things Aparna sees on the way. People in this city are self-sufficient. They have grown organic vegetables, fruits, and herbs in their own gardens. People are also taught to use their waste material. Transportation here is very advanced. Flying scooters, Autonomous offline taxis, electric buses, and high-speed bullet trains run here. Aparna can see them in front of her eyes. Vasu tells her that accidents hardly ever happen here. Robots can also be seen everywhere.

Vasu tells Aparna that people receive medical checkups and treatment from their own homes. In addition, every person's health profile is in digital form, allowing doctors to diagnose and treat them correctly. Vasu tells Aparna about life here, where technological advancement is quite high. This includes self-driving cars, artificial intelligence, and advanced medical treatment. This is common knowledge.

Aparna is looking at the music track's name on the car's screen. The name of the music track is "Robot Lovers", a song about crossing the boundary between humans and machines. It explores the possibility of falling in love with machines, like humans. Aparna is enjoying this song.

Aparna: when technology has advanced so much, who is what here? Are there humans, or machines, and what are we?

Vasu: if I say that you are a machine, then you won't be able to differentiate. You are in a world where humans can live forever with advanced medical treatment and digital immortality.

You may remember I told you that there have been many studies on stem cells, bio computers and brainwaves. Just understand that the result of that study is this world. We discovered this world many years ago. At first, research was done on the nature and states of brainwaves. What can we make from their effects, there is a direct connection between brainwaves and the state of consciousness. Like their relative relationship with wakefulness, sleep, meditation, and samadhi.

Just like the tools you have there, such as EEG, MEG, and fMRI... are all very basic. They are great for exploring. There are wonders and mysteries in this universe. In fact, we have more than one universe and dimension with us. Each person in it has their own set of physical laws and properties for each universe. In their own way, each universe interacts with each other in ways that are beyond our current understanding.

Aparna, could you simplify this for me? It's another planet. I'm in a dream, what is this?

Vasu, look at it this way. Every event can have an alternate reality, where different choices can lead to different outcomes. For example, right now we are driving on a straight road. This is the current event. But if we stop the car and start walking back, and then come back and sit in the car and drive straight again, both outcomes will be different. In one, we will reach home quickly and in the other, we will reach home a little later.

Similarly, every activity we do has multiple choices, but we always live and experience only one possibility at a time. So, we are only living one possibility at a time, but all the possibilities that we could have lived exist.

I told you that we never die. We live through all possibilities. Right now, we are in the possibility where the machine age has arrived. In fact, this place has been recreated fully. Life was on the brink of ending here. But we have recreated it in an entirely new way.

Aparna, are you telling me that we are currently in a parallel world? And I am your wife here? I understand, but why did you bring me here? By the way, tell me the truth. I am asking some questions, but I do not even feel like asking anything... I am not even sure what to ask... This is a dream, but it is very beautiful if it is true. The weather here is so pleasant. Vasu smiles looking at Aparna and says, "I can understand your feelings."

As they talk, they both reach home where there is a robot that does all the work in the house. It cooks food and is available 24/7 for any needs. Vasu tells Aparna that the robot's name is Tiago. Aparna looks around and sees that it is a magnificent and luxurious house called "The Oasis".

The architecture is very modern. High-tech materials have been used in its exterior that not only make its structure strong but also enhance its look. Its entrance is also very luxurious, with splendid places throughout. There are extra furnishings as well. The highlight of the house is its large indoor swimming pool, which provides a private office experience only in one's own home. There is a sunbathing area near the pool where one can also enjoy summer drinks. There is also a large garden outside the house, with exotic plants and flowers. There are four bedrooms inside the house, each with an attached bathroom that has high-end bath fittings. Along with that, there is a magnificent living room, fully equipped kitchen, dining room, media room, and gym inside. Vasu tells Aparna about the house's advanced security system and informs her about all the features and splendid lifestyle.

The Feelings Of Love

While talking, Vasu looks into Aparna's eyes and holds her hand, and says, "All of this is ours." Aparna was feeling overwhelmed at that moment. It felt like life had given her everything all at once. Vasu takes Aparna towards the bedroom where there is also a photo of Vasu and Aparna.

Aparna: If I am your wife, then why don't I remember anything? And if my body here is dead, what was the reason for my death?

Vasu: I will tell you everything and explain it to you. Just give yourself some time. First, freshen up a bit and spend some time with me. I have not told you before, but you have been here for almost 21 days. So, give yourself and me at least one week. You said earlier that you feel like you are in a dream, right? So, consider this a dream for now.

Saying this, Vasu approaches Aparna and leans in to kiss her, but Aparna pushes him back a bit and says, "Okay, but you also give me some time. If this is really a dream and I am this conscious in the dream, then it is difficult for me to suddenly see you as my husband. Please understand."

However, while saying this, Vasu hugs Aparna again and says, "I have been waiting for you for a long time. So, I can't resist now. You understand. And just remember that I am your husband." Aparna does not stop Vasu this time and now she does not say anything. Her silence is her yes. She also felt very peaceful in Vasu's arms. They stay embraced in each other's arms for a while.

Vasu: "Listen, will you have some tea?"

Aparna: "Yes, I would definitely like to have some tea."

They both go towards the kitchen. Vasu is making tea. Aparna notices that the kitchen still has some basic utensils made of clay and a normal stove beside the electronic gas stove.

Aparna: "These clay utensils?"

Before Aparna could complete her sentence, Vasu speaks, "This is all because of your wish. This is nothing. I will show you more."

Vasu serves tea in two cups after making it. Aparna and Vasu both take one cup of tea each and holding the cups in their hands, they go to the terrace according to Vasu's instructions.

The terrace is open and has a traditional kitchen with a mud stove, brass utensils, and a mortar and pestle for making chutneys, along with several other old things that Aparna had always dreamed of having in her dream home. Vasu tells her that Aparna made all these things.

Aparna drinks the most perfect tea she has ever had while standing in her dream home and admiring the new city from all sides.

They keep talking for a long time. As they talk, they gradually come closer to each other. Vasu touches and kisses Aparna repeatedly, answering her questions. Vasu is introducing Aparna to this new world.

After talking for a long time on the terrace, Aparna and Vasu return to the bedroom.

Vasu says, "Let's take a shower together."

Aparna thinks for a few seconds and then says yes.

She is feeling the warm steam emanating from the elegant bathroom of the luxurious villa where they are staying with Vasu, which creates a dim, hazy atmosphere around them. The sound of falling water echoes in her ears and her body is enveloped in the fragrance of the scented shower gel.

Aparna's mind is now empty of any thoughts, and she is completely in the present moment.

Both come out after taking a shower. Aparna looks at the wardrobe and sees a collection she never even dreamt of. Vasu selects a white dress for Aparna and helps her get ready.

Both get ready and head toward the dining area. Tiago has already set the breakfast table, which has fresh juice, vegetables, Aparna's favorite besan chilla, and many varieties of food.

Aparna notices that Vasu is quite conscious while choosing his breakfast. Both finish their breakfast. Aparna already feels better.

Vasu: you have come here for the first time then you need to get a feel for the environment, let's roam around a bit today.

Aparna interrupts Vasu's voice in the middle and says, "First, you explain and tell me everything so that I can also enjoy all of this correctly."

Vasu replies, "If you give me some time, then I won't need to explain everything to you. Please give me some time."

Vasu lovingly holds Aparna's hand and says, "I know you have many questions in your mind, but at least give me two to three days."

Aparna: okay. So, I will not ask these things.

Please don't give me the answer to big questions, just answer the small ones, like whether you have any family members like relatives, mother, father, brother, sister or not.......... I have not seen anyone looking at their mobile phones here. So how do you all communicate with each other?

Vasu: So..yes, I don't have anybody other than you…I have some friends and we will meet them soon… there is a kind of communication here, plantable devices play an important role in it. …These are bio-electronic devices that are implanted as neural implants. These devices interface with the brain or nervous system inside the body, allowing two bodies to communicate directly with each other. These devices are also implanted in your body. Their use is not yet active. When your body enters a relaxed state, some specific hormones will be released. After that, you will gradually feel more sensitivity. By tomorrow morning, you will not have so many questions. You will understand this place quite well.

Aparna: "Okay, fine, all right. I'm starting to understand a little bit. Let us leave it. Let's enjoy ourselves today. This is all so amazing.

(Aparna was feeling a little scared too, afraid that her old life might catch up to her. She was also confused because some things were fitting logically for her, while others weren't. But this world was so beautiful that it was like heaven to her.)

Vasu takes Aparna on a flying scooter this time, which is available on every corner of the city. They pick it up from multiple locations and drop it off at any other station. People here use this mode of public transportation the most. They were flying about 30 feet above the ground and it was so smooth that it was like they were not even on the road. It was like a train running on an invisible track. After about half an hour of flying, they park it at a station and continue on foot from there."

Vasu is talking to Aparna about electronic money. He talks about the shape of the social structure, technological, economic, political, and cultural. He says that the traditional family structure is very rare here. He speaks about acceptance regarding alternative family structures - single parents, households, and same-gender couples.

He told her that there are many food chain brands available there with slightly changed names.

Vasu also explains that both worlds are connected in such a way that whenever a brand name's share market rises here, the share of the brand-related product falls there. This is quite complex and interesting, and most things are automatic. India is ahead of all countries in the world here. There is a world-famous university here where people from all over the world come to study.

Aparna: I guess… like me, some other people have also settled in this parallel world in their second body.

Vasu: yes, many people keep coming here. Some people are frequent travelers here. No matter how many famous celebrities you see in your world, all their clones are here. It is people's fantasy to be in their bodies here.

This is not the only parallel world. There are many such worlds here. Consistently, very few people come here. Most people come here after death. Some travelers are addicted to drugs. Whenever someone gets a signal here, they reach some parallel world by moving a little away from their body's time and space. Many times, the people here take advantage of the unconscious people and bring them here. And when those people return to their bodies, they don't even remember anything special.

As Aparna talks, she sees the whole city, and it's almost noon. Aparna really likes this new Delhi city. Aparna has traveled to five or six countries outside of India, but this was even better than that. She felt like she was on a dream date.

Vasu: let's go, it's time for lunch. I'll take you to your favorite restaurant, Sanskriti.

Vasu takes Aparna to a restaurant called "Sanskriti". The look and feel of this restaurant were completely different. It was a mix of innovative design, modern technology, traditional Indian architecture, and decor.

As they entered the restaurant, a modern reception desk, and friendly robots welcomed them. Their booking details were checked there. Facial recognition technology was used to enter the restaurant.

Aparna observed the restaurant's environment, which was filled with traditional Indian colors, decors, and brightly colored artistic lighting. The table had an interactive menu system where one could easily order their dishes. Aparna ordered an Indian thali, and with the help of small robots, the food was served perfectly.

Aparna was feeling that her taste buds had increased by more than 50% at this time while eating. She had never tasted food so deliciously before. She could not think about anything else while eating. The chefs were preparing food at the live cooking station in the restaurant, and musical performances and traditional dance shows were going on. They were providing a full dose of entertainment. Aparna enjoyed her delicious and spicy platter filled with colorful Indian dishes. After that, she sipped the cool mango lassi and enjoyed the music.

After that, they went out again to roam around. Vasu showed Aparna some screens where you can touch and there are all kinds of information on these screens. There were also some headsets with which you can experience GPS, virtual reality, and movie-like experiences.

She did not know how time was passing there. Some things were very common that she had seen before, and some things were very special. Vasu took Aparna to a garden. This garden was also unique.

Aparna's eyes sparkled with joy at the sight of fragrant flowers, sparkling fountains, and magnificent views. There were many trees and plants underneath which digital screens were placed with all their information. Vasu held Aparna's hand and walked her around the entire garden. After walking for a while, he signaled her to sit next to him on a flat round pedestal. Aparna sat near him. Vasu kept staring at Aparna. The sun was setting, casting a warm glow over the garden.

Vasu, do you know how special you are to me? I feel alive only when I'm close to you. There is a special bond between us.

Aparna was listening to Vasu's words, but her eyes could not move away from the beauty of the garden, surrounded by captivating marble fountains and lush greenery.

As Vasu spoke, he brought his face closer to Aparna's, and her heartbeat quickened. She felt a surge of excitement in her stomach. She looked into Vasu's eyes, thinking that he was the only man she wanted to spend her life with.

Without saying anything, Vasu approached Aparna and lightly kissed her on the lips, causing Aparna to feel a cool sensation on her spine. As she got closer to Vasu, she felt even more sensations in his body. After pausing there for a while, Vasu and Aparna went home.

It was already 8:00 pm and the weather had become slightly chilly.

Vasu: what would you like to eat for dinner? I have an idea, but I still want to ask you.

Aparna: Something light. Lunch was already too heavy.

Vasu smiles and says "Already knew that.'

He gave instructions to his Robot Tiago and takes Aparna back to the bedroom.

Aparna notices that Vasu does not want her to be alone even for a short while. She does not even get a chance to think about anything.

Aparna: I want to take a bath again, but alone this time. Please? I did not have enough time to shower this morning, and I was feeling shy. Let me enjoy my privacy.

"Okay, okay, my love. I will get the bathtub ready for you," Vasu responds.

After a few minutes, Aparna was enjoying the bathtub and was feeling the warmth of the water. She was suddenly hit by the realization of the unexpected changes in her lifestyle. It was as if one memory had shifted into another. In just one day, it felt like her old life was slipping away. Lost in thought, she heard the bathroom gate sliding open

Vasu comes inside, smiling, and lies down in the tub with Aparna.

Aparna: "You don't respect my privacy, do you? You have come here too?"

Vasu: "You're doing okay, for now, good or bad. Please stop thinking about all this. Wherever you come from, I have seen your life.

I can't see you like this anymore, and I can't wait for you here for ages. Do you even know how much I've waited for you here? And as for privacy, so…. Tomorrow morning, you won't talk about all these things. I promise you. Loosen up a bit.

Aparna: look Vasu…, I can agree with everything you say. But I cannot change my nature or my personality.

The situation now is that I really want to stay here. I want to believe everything you say. I want to believe in what I see, hear, and feel here. But I am still afraid…. My physical senses are telling me something else…. You are lying beside me and kissing me in this way, and I also want to move forward…. But I am afraid.

Aparna was speaking but he ignores her words and kisses her lips in between. And they both get lost in each other for a long time. Aparna still tries to stop herself and does not let Vasu go further.

Vasu, how long will you hold yourself back? And why are you stopping me?

"I'm not understanding anything at the moment," she says,

Her heart beat fast. She walks out of the bathroom in a few moments. Vasu also comes out and hugs Aparna, saying, "Don't worry, I won't force you for anything. But trust me, this is important."

Afterward, Vasu takes Aparna to the garden of the house for dinner. The stars are shining in the sky, and there is soft music playing. There is a round table, two chairs, two wine glasses, a wine bottle, and a covered plate placed on the table. Along with that, a robot named Tiago is standing.

Aparna: Wow, what is going on? What is for dinner?

Vasu asks Tiago to serve dinner.

Vasu: We've made some fresh vegetables and paneer fries. You will love it.

Aparna: There you were making me meditate, and now you want to give me wine?

Vasu: Yes, it is important to serve wine. (Saying this, Vasu looks mischievously at Aparna)

Aparna remains silent and simply lifts her wine glass and touches it with Vasu's glass. She takes a big sip and they both eat and continue to talk. After that, they both stroll in the garden for a while.

Aparna: everything is changing so quickly, it's amazing. I don't know what kind of feeling it is, there's fear and excitement. There is also a little guilt. Everything has mixed. There is also a slight buzz on top of it. I never thought something like this would happen in my life...but it is okay.

Vasu: just chill, man.... What happened to you? Is my company that bad?

Aparna: no. There is nothing like that. Today has been the best day of my life so far with you.

Vasu: do not overthink and just think about me a little.

(Vasu holds Aparna's hand and puts it on his chest, showing his heartbeat. His heart rate is quite fast and his breaths are getting faster.)

Aparna: I am thinking about you.

Vasu: I will not be able to sleep without your physical touch. I need it badly, in fact, we both need it.

Aparna had never heard these things from her husband Vijay in her old life. She never felt that Vijay needed her, and here she is in a completely opposite situation where Vasu is standing in front of her.

There, she could not say anything that came to her mind. Because before that, Vasu grabs her tightly and starts kissing her on the lips.

Aparna was surprised by Vasu's sudden action. She had never expected him to grab her like that and start kissing her passionately. But as his lips moved on hers, she found herself responding to him in ways she never knew she could. Her heart was beating fast and her breathing became heavy as he continued to kiss her. Before she knew it, Vasu had lifted her up in his arms and was carrying her toward the bedroom. Aparna's mind was in a daze, but she could not resist the strong pull that Vasu had on her. As they entered the bedroom, Vasu gently placed Aparna on the bed and continued to kiss her. Aparna had always been reserved and hesitant in expressing her desires, but with Vasu, she felt liberated. She let go of all her inhibitions and allowed herself to be completely lost in the moment. The two of them were completely consumed by their passion, as they explored each other's bodies and reveled in the intensity of their love. Hours went by, but Aparna and Vasu were lost in their own world. For the first time in a long time, Aparna felt truly happy and content. As they lay in each other's arms, she realized that she had finally found the love that she had been searching for all her life. And in Vasu, she had found the one person who could make her feel truly alive.

Aparna felt something for the first time in her life. She had never felt this kind of physical touch before. Now, for the first time, she was feeling satisfied. She did not know when she fell asleep after that. She just cuddled up and slept.

The next day when Aparna woke up, everything had changed for her. She was able to feel herself on the left side of her body, and feel Vasu on the right side of her body. She could feel Vasu's heartbeat, the flow of his emotions, and the current thoughts that were running through her mind. Everything was known to her.

Vasu was making tea for Aparna in the kitchen. and Aparna knew her location too. She was able to sense what Vasu was feeling while making tea. It felt as if Aparna was Vasu herself. This was a unique connection. She felt her own body very sensitive and felt a deep mutual trust in Vasu's hands. It seemed that their relationship had become even deeper. In a few moments, Vasu comes back with tea.

Vasu: what you are feeling right now is called the bond between the soul and the atom. I don't need to explain to you what I'm feeling now. Even when you weren't here, we were still connected. At that time, you could not feel me in this way. Because of this bond, we can smell each other's body's diseases. We can fix them. We will always be connected, consciously and unconsciously.

Aparna was silently listening to Vasu's words. With each sentence, she wondered what he was feeling. While speaking, Aparna was also able to feel along with him. It was a magical moment.

After that, Aparna did not even realize how a week went by. For the first time, she felt what it means to be together. She had only heard the term "perfect couple" before, but now she understood its true meaning. Vasu taught and showed Aparna about different things and ways there every day. This magical place had now become a new truth for Aparna in every way.

This place is called Alpha Earth. The time is March 2050. There is no place for any religious institution, such as temples, mosques, or churches. It is difficult to distinguish between machines and humans. Things that look like humans and have high emotions have profound experiences. People never die here. They live until their wishes are fulfilled. After that, their memories are transferred through a new memory chip to a new body. Then they experience their experiences again.

Vasu says, "There are many worlds that are connected to this Alpha Earth and direct trade takes place between them. Some of them have slightly lower ethics and value systems because they use their technology to exploit the people of Earth for their own benefit. There, machines experience their five senses through them."

Therefore, a major epidemic hit the Earth every 30-40 years and many people die. In your world where people are often influenced by the influential people of that world in their activities. They can make them think according to their own brain waves, which allows them to make them dance as they want.

Vasu tells that even on Alpha Earth, there was once an invasion of artificial intelligence and technology. At that time, humans created another human, but the artificially created humans, called "Hymnths," were unable to carry emotions like humans. Their brain was faster than 100 computers, and their body was much stronger. After some time, they enslaved humans. The natural birth of humans on this planet came to a halt. During that time, they discovered many worlds like theirs and found some help from them. Since then, every world has been learning from each other.

In one week, Vasu showed Aparna the university, the library, and the shopping malls here. The learning process is going on here with great enthusiasm. Vasu introduced Aparna to many of his friends. They had a party on a cruise.

Exploring the New

Now it was time for Aparna to see the lab that Vasu keeps mentioning repeatedly.

Aparna goes to the lab with Vasu. From the outside, it looked like a normal building. But upon entering, the basement was so large that an entire small city could fit inside it. The lab has different sections. Vasu takes Aparna to a section called Cortex Connect. There was a device that looked like a helmet, which Vasu explains has invasive sensors that can measure the electrical activity of the brain. The data obtained is transmitted to a computer system, which analyzes the data. The unconscious brain provides the data to the computer. The freezer data is also analyzed, and this data can be viewed like a movie in memory. Through Cortex Connect, Alpha Earth people can also pass messages to their companion partners on Earth.

This lab has machines that also provide brain training exercises to increase human focus, memory, and attention. There are brain-developing computer interfaces here, through which communication is established between the brain and external devices, which can also control prosthetic limbs, virtual reality systems, and other technologies.

Here, the human body can be scanned and analyzed to repair its damaged parts.

This involves the use of advanced robotics, nanotechnology, and biotechnology.

The different sections of the lab are dedicated to specific aspects and processes. The technology in this lab is so advanced that artificial human beings can be created. Different sections work on different things, such as designing and building machines in one section, and robotic mechanical engineering and automation staff in another section.

There are also experienced scientists and engineers in the latter section. One team of scientists works on genetic sequencing and engineering of human DNA. The other team works on developing and testing design traits and value systems. There is a separate staff for developing and testing different types of tissue engineering.

At Alpha earth regenerative medicine techniques are common. In this technique, human beings repair their organs and tissues themselves. The lab has a highly advanced AI system. The entire process from start to finish is managed by AI and programmed. Due to this AI-based machine learning program, a large amount of data is analyzed, and the real-time decision process is working successfully.

(Aparna was listening, watching, and observing all of this without saying a word. She had never seen anything like this in her life before.)

After this, Vasu takes Aparna to a part of the lab where Alpha Earth's scientist, was watching the people of Earth on a big high-tech screen. At that time, Aparna noticed that a matchmaking process was going on one screen, like on a matrimonial website. She saw a man sitting in front of the screen searching for compatibility for an Alpha Earth boy. He was searching for a girl on Earth who had all kinds of compatibility. Aparna did not understand this.

Aparna asks Vasu, "Vasu, what's going on? If people from Earth cannot come here, then why this match-making?"

Vasu explains, "Aparna, this match-making is actually happening with the memory of a human. The memory is copied into a memory chip and then transmitted into an artificial human body, creating all emotions and value systems through that memory chip. This process takes about six months. During this time, the artificial human body is kept in an intensive care unit, where surgical risks, recovery, and physical, and mental health are taken care of. After that, the one who is made for that boy will be taken with him."

Aparna: it sounds very strange to hear this. In this way, humans are only like a product here.

Vasu: That's not true. In Alpha, only one life partner can be created in one life. Divorce does not happen here like on Earth. Every resident on Alpha chooses only one partner and spends their entire life with them. Only in one case can a life partner be changed, if your life partner no longer desires to live and chooses death. The decision to end their life independently can be made on Alpha. After making such a decision, the person must go through a process, and if the A.I. report is okay, methods such as a lethal dose of medication and participating in physician-assisted suicide are completed. Those who are left behind can choose their partner again.

Aparna: I do not understand. This is very strange.

Vasu: I can understand. I can feel your emotions and feelings inside you right now.

I told you that life had ended here. The people who survived did not have the same human emotions left as on your Earth, so we didn't have much optimism among us. We were just trying to find a balance between machines and humans. And we have been quite successful to a great extent. All decisions here are made by AI, and there is no room for any kind of unfairness. There is a system here that is equal for everyone.

Aparna: Was I also made the same way here?

Vasu: Yes. Right now, our bodies are connected. You can feel what emotions I am carrying with me. If I had told you this before, you would not have understood it. It may seem artificial to see, but for me, it is true and I am living in this truth. There is a complete life thriving here on Alpha Earth.

Aparna: I have not seen any cremation ground since coming here. Obviously, all the organs of the bodies would be reused here.

Do people also take Mahasamadhi here?

Vasu: Yes, they do. There is another place where I will take you today.

Aparna says, "you told me that my body had died here. Why did that happen? How could my will to live end here when everything I wanted was here? Why did I leave? If I left, why didn't you choose another partner at that time?"

Vasu responds, "No one can know why someone's will to live ends. It's an independent decision that depends on multiple things. After you left, I was alone here for a long time. Our compatibility was 95%, which is the highest compatibility on Alpha Earth so far. We are a record of ourselves. I always wanted a child, but you never did. I wanted us to have a child delivered naturally on Alpha

Earth. But you mostly focused on your research here. Nevertheless, we were very happy. But that 5% gap between you and me became dominant over our 95% compatibility.

And one day, you insisted on going to the "Elysian Garden," a place where people meditate and attain a state of samadhi, leaving behind their physical body and residing in their subtle body without any physical presence. You never returned from there.

I had only one way, we were building a machine at that time which could help the subtle body travel to any place leaving the physical body behind. I dived into that research as soon as the machine was ready. And then I started looking for different possibilities for you. Before this travel, I also went to "Elysian Garden". There, I received help from my ancestors who have already become Nemo. A yogi ancestor of mine helped me to find you. He told me which possibility could bring you here.

We are going to "Elysian Garden" now; you will learn a lot by seeing it.

Aparna: by the way, what is your age?

Vasu: approximately 458 years and 7 months.

Aparna: it is amazing. Even after living for so many years, your desire to live has not ended yet. How long have we been together?

Vasu: approximately 7 years.

Aparna: that means you mostly spend your time alone.

Vasu: yes. My parents were killed during the machine age invasion. After that, my grandfather took care of me and raised me. At that time, only a few humans were left. We received help from some other parallel worlds, and today this organized automatic system is a result of that. My grandfather was a great scientist, but we didn't know that he was also a great yogi. His entire life was devoted to exploring human mental abilities. But in the last days of his life, he changed completely. Most of his time was spent in meditation. After that, he went to Elysian Garden and took samadhi. His physical body was destroyed there, but he is still sitting there with his subtle body. Now he has also become a Nemo.

Vasu gently places his hand on Aparna's cheek and said ". I am sensing what you are feeling right now. What are you experiencing now? That's why it was necessary for us to spend time together in the beginning to understand all of this."

Aparna became completely silent as she heard all of this. Her mind was filled with many questions. Experiencing so many new things and accepting them was not easy.

After that, Vasu took Aparna through an underground tunnel that led to a very large open ground. In front of her was a circular entrance from where very bright light was coming. After crossing that entrance, there was a very large forest with big old trees. The jungle was quite deep. Vasu pointed to Aparna and indicated that this was the garden.

The vibrations of that place were completely different. The jungle was completely untouched. She had never seen such big trees before. Each tree was very tall, with a thick trunk and roots sticking out.

Vasu explained that this place is considered very sacred by everyone here. People come here only when all their science fails. Their ancestors reside here in a subtle form and help the residents from time to time. Most people come here towards the end of their lives. This happens when someone gets a disease for which we don't have a cure. So, we do meditation with the patient sitting here. Nemo comes into their body and treats them. This place is very mysterious. Nemo is not easily visible here. They don't let everyone come inside. Only the person whom Nemo wants to help can enter.

Aparna: Can we see them?

Vasu: Yes, maybe some of them.

Vasu gives Aparna a pair of glasses to wear. When Aparna looks towards the jungle through those glasses, she sees many red-colored transparent structures, mostly shining like small suns under the trees.

Aparna: Can they see and hear us?

Vasu: Yes, not just us, they can see and hear everything. Their reach is limitless. They know everything. They meet us through dreams continuously

Many times, whenever we try to contact these people, they come forward to help. This place is very magnificent. There are many mysteries in this place for which science has no answer. Sometimes sudden changes occur in the bodies of observant people. Their physical abilities become much better than ordinary people's. Such people are also brought here. Just as Alpha Earth Fourth Dimension is for Earth, there is a way here for other dimensions that are in the middle of this place. It appears to be ordinary stairs at first glance, but special physical abilities are necessary to climb those stairs.

Their world is quite different from ours. They also correct our mistakes from time to time and serve as a link between different worlds.

The experience of connecting with Nemo is truly remarkable and each person's experience is unique. It's fascinating to note that most women who meditate are able to easily establish this connection. The mechanics of how this works remain a mystery to me. However, on Alpha Earth, the male and female bodies are already inherently connected. When the female body establishes its connection in accordance with certain rules, we place the male body in a state of "Cortex Connect" and can receive the same information that the female body is experiencing. Regrettably, this connection is not sustainable for an extended period.

When you were last there, we were the first couple to have sustained this connection for the longest time. It was then that we discovered what the ascent up these stairs entails. There is a total of seven dimensions present, which can be thought of as seven floors. After traversing each floor, the experience becomes increasingly profound. At this point, the gravitational force on the body becomes so intense that the physical body is fragmented into minuscule particles. This is known as the Nemo state, but even after entering this state, life persists.

After this, those who still have learning left, live around these trees only. Others continue to climb up these stairs. As they go up each floor, they receive a new body. Life on each floor is completely different. Physical abilities are different. Experiences are different. Everyone wants to go to the upper floors from the lower floors.

But not everyone can go, everyone gets different types of powers on this journey. The oldest Nemo here is my great-grandfather, who has been here for thousands of years. We often receive help from him.

Aparna: have you ever felt like you could feel other dimensions? That you could go to a different world than the one you live in?

Vasu looks at Aparna with love and responds, "You are my world. If I haven't even explored this world yet, how could I even think of wanting to see any other world?"

"I am currently figuring out a way for you to permanently stay here with me and we can live our lives together.

Aparna: does that mean I won't be able to go back now?"

Vasu: do you want to leave?"

Aparna: No, that's not it. But it feels strange. My parents, siblings. And Vijay will have to live without me?

Vasu: Even if you die for some reason there, they still must live without you, right? Do you know how much time is left for you there?

Aparna: What does that mean? Does being there mean I'm going to die there?

Vasu: In every possibility, your death happens at the age of 39. So anyway, you have only 7 years left there. I went out for several years to find you here. Now, I want to live with you.

Aparna: You know how to send me back, right?

Vasu: Yes, I do.

Aparna: Before coming here, I want to meet my family again.

Vasu: Yes, I can understand that.

After that, both went back home.

And The Learning Goes On

They were both having tea in the evening. Aparna: I'm feeling a little guilty about Vijay. Vasu: There's no need for that. Do you have any idea what he's up to? Why isn't he around you? The world doesn't stop for anyone's coming or going. It just keeps moving. So, don't feel guilty about anything. You are where you should be. Aparna felt a little lost that evening. Vasu could sense her sadness.

At night, Vasu tries to get closer to Aparna in the bedroom, but Aparna refuses. Upon this, Vasu says, "Your dopamine levels are decreasing. That's why you're feeling sad. Please let me come closer to you.

Aparna's response was filled with anger, "You're speaking like a machine. I'm feeling like a complete fool right now. Be it this world or any other, one has to accept the surroundings. I don't even have a proper understanding of myself."

Vasu says, "Hey, calm down baby. I understand your feelings right now. Take your own time. Okay? I am right here with you."

Aparna doesn't say anything for a while. After a few moments of silence,

Aparna asks, "Do you still want a child?"

Vasu replies, "No, I just want you now.

Aparna: Have you become accustomed to my habits?

Vasu: We were made to live with each other.

Aparna: If that's the case, then the person you created wasn't me, right? That Aparna was a different individual entity here. And I am a completely different person.

This dual life is very strange. I don't understand anything.... Can I recover my memory? Can I see my past life?

Vasu: We could never copy any of your memories. You were brought here just like this before. That's why we are the most compatible couple. However, there are some video clips and some of your research work, and some recordings that are available on Cortex connect. If you want, you can watch them.

Aparna: Okay, so from tomorrow, I want to start working on my research work again. We will go to the regular lab tomorrow. We should start work again.

Vasu: We have a lot of time for that. Right now, you are here for a little while. Once you go back and come here again, then you and I will be here forever.

Aparna: This whole Maya-Jal (illusionary trap) is completely new for me to understand. I don't want to stay with half-knowledge.

Vasu: Okay, we'll do as you wish. All right? So please come to me now.

In this way, the night passes too. The next day, Aparna and Vasu go to the lab.

Vasu connects Aparna with the lab staff. He introduces her to the team she was previously working with. The most senior person in that team is named Raman.

All the information that Aparna had received so far was only through Vasu. Now Aparna wanted to gather some new information.

Vasu leaves Aparna at the lab with her team and both attend to their respective tasks. On the same day, Raman takes Aparna to a part of the lab where he explains to her the concept of parallel worlds and time.

There was a very large screen there, on which there was a sphere that looked like the Earth. There was a core written on it. Raman clicks on the sphere. As soon as he touches it, a time start appears on the sphere, which was the present time, 10:25 am. In front of it, another sphere started emerging from the same sphere, in which time was running in a decreasing series. In the same way, in a short time, the entire screen was filled. Raman clicks on the spheres randomly one by one. Aparna sees that in one place, they were standing in the exact same condition. Aparna and Raman were talking to each other. Clicking on the second sphere plays a second video on the screen, in which Aparna was standing in another part of the lab

Aparna asked Raman in surprise, "What is all this?" Raman replied, "These are your possibilities in the present time, Madam." Aparna questioned, "How many such possibilities are there?" Raman answered, "It is infinite, Madam. And each one has its own individuality of Aparna. AI has created all of this." Aparna asked again, "Did Vasu get the possibility of being on my Earth from here?"

Raman, yes, Madam. But this machine only shows possibilities, not locations. To travel to the live location of that possibility, one must travel with a subtle body through infinite possibilities. We get help from Nemo for that. Just like Vasu got help to find you.

Aparna asks, can we see anyone's possibility here?

Raman explains, yes, you can see their possibility if it's in your memory. Besides that, to see the possibilities of anyone else, you must fulfill some legal formalities. You need to have some solid reasons for that.

Aparna asks, "Can I see my family on my Earth live?" Raman answers, "Yes, anytime. I'll show you now." Raman takes Aparna to the Cortex Connect and gives her a helmet-like device. He also puts a glass-like gadget on her eyes.

Raman politely requests, "Madam, if you could wait for just 30 seconds? Then, you can go wherever you desire based on your thoughts."

Within a short while, Aparna catches a glimpse of her family and spots Vijay. She also witnesses the possibility that she passes away and Vijay moves on with ease. This sight relieves her of all her guilt.

Just moments later, the machine comes to an abrupt halt with a jolt. Aparna suddenly feels a wave of exhaustion washing over her body, as if she has just exerted herself to the limit.

Raman smiles reassuringly and says, "It's normal to feel this way the first time you use it. Let me get you some juice."

After a short while, Vasu returns with the juice in hand. He lovingly places his hand on Aparna's head and hands her the juice, reassuring her that it's okay not to grasp everything in one day.

Aparna inquires, "Vasu, do you have something to hide from me?"

Vasu responds, "The things here are vastly different from Earth, and I'm simply concerned that you don't lose your mental balance while attempting to learn them too quickly."

Aparna spends the entire day trying to understand the concepts of time, space, and the maze. She watches her old video clips, looks at her research and talks to other people. She is busy with her things all day. It was almost 8:00 at night and almost all the staff had left. Vasu kept insisting Aparna go home repeatedly.

After Vasu's repeated insistence, Aparna finally agrees to leave. She gathers her things and prepares to go home. As she walks out of the building, she looks up at the stars and wonders how different they must look from this place.

Despite feeling exhausted, Aparna is excited to continue exploring this new world and learning more about its unique concepts.

After the long day, Vasu, and Aparna return home, with Aparna remaining silent on the way back. From then on, Aparna's learning process becomes increasingly intense day by day

After spending nearly 19 days on the Alpha planet and acquiring valuable knowledge, Aparna expressed her desire to connect with Nemo before leaving for Earth. Despite Vasu's repeated attempts to discourage her, she remained resolute.

Ultimately, Vasu accompanied Aparna to Elysian Garden where they stood at the entrance gate.

Concerned about the potential dangers to her Earthly body, Vasu cautioned Aparna, "This is risky. Please reconsider."

But Aparna replied firmly, "I have already thought about it."

Aparna says this and moves ahead. Vasu walks with her and gestures toward a tree. "And it's here."

Aparna walks towards the tree and goes underneath it. Vasu lays out a yoga mat there and signals for Aparna to sit down.

Vasu: As per the protocol, I need to go to the Cortex connect in the lab for brainwave reading. But it is okay, you can stay here.

"I'll join you soon," Aparna spoke, expressing her gratitude towards Vasu's presence.

After Vasu left, Aparna settled down to meditate. The ambiance of the jungle was unfamiliar to her, yet she tried to establish a connection with Nemo, following Vasu's advice

Despite half an hour passing, Aparna did not feel any different. Meanwhile, in the lab, Raman and the other staff chatted amongst themselves, wondering if Aparna would be able to establish the connection. Most people doubted her ability, but Raman and Vasu were certain that she will.

Aparna closes her eyes and silently invokes, "I call upon the power that permeates every particle, the force that drives life in every being, the source of all movement. I acknowledge this power as Shiva and also as Nemo. Please, connect with me and guide me toward the right path. Show me only the purpose of my presence here, and reveal to me only what I need to know. I surrender myself completely and seek your assistance. Please, connect with me."

After a while, Aparna finds herself in emptiness, where there is only her and nothing else. She feels like she is one with life. She does not feel anything. For a few moments, there is no memory. She does not know where she is sitting.

Meanwhile, chaos erupts in the lab on the other side. Raman shouts, "I had said she will do it. She is different." Everyone was running toward their respective screens. Vasu was slowly transitioning from conscious to semi-conscious and from semi-conscious to unconscious state.

Raman was surprised to see that the coding and decoding speed running on the brain wave reading machine attached to Vasu was very high. He had never seen such speed before. On the other hand, Aparna had already entered the astral world. After staying in the void for a while, she enters the same state that Vasu had described.

Vasu had told Aparna that in this situation, the logical mind remains less active. Whenever Nemo connects, the person gets lost in a story. The person sitting there remains lost in that story, while on the other side, the coding recording of that story runs in the lab, and is decoded later. This information provides a lot of information to the Alpha Earth residents and using that information, new research is conducted there. New types of machines are made, and gadgets are created.

People are free to ask anything they desire and one can acquire knowledge about anything. This was evident on that day when Raman and the staff posed numerous inquiries, exploring the promising avenues of regenerative medicine and nanotechnology.

The sheer excitement was palpable, as it marked a defining moment in their lives. The team was able to capture the live location of multiple parallel worlds they had been engaged with for years, all within a single day. everyone was surprised that despite so much happening, the connection was still maintained.

After almost 4 hours, Vasu suddenly got up. He asked Raman, "Is everything all right?"

Raman replied, "Yes sir, everything is wonderful.

This was the best so far. Let me decode the fully coated information and then you can go to madam."

Vasu simply gets up and drinks a glass of water before leaving to pick up Aparna. The rest of the staff is also standing there at the gate, watching Aparna from a distance.

After a while, Vasu reaches the Elysian Garden. He notices the staff standing there, checking the IMF machine with worried expressions. One of the men among them explains that the electromagnetic signal has been lost. Vasu takes a gadget resembling a telescope from one of the men

And he looks at Aparna from afar. Aparna was still sitting there with her eyes closed. Vasu was thinking about approaching Aparna when one of the staff members said, "It could be very dangerous to disturb her in the middle of the process. You know the rules." Restless, Vasu was just watching Aparna from there.

About an hour pass, but Aparna remains unaffected by the commotion. A new IMF machine is brought in. Everyone tries to maintain the signal again. Meanwhile, Aparna's last message is decoded in the lab. Upon learning of it, Raman becomes anxious and immediately connects with Vasu.

Vasu learns that Aparna is going to travel in the Higher Dimensions, where no one has gone before. The dimension is still mysterious and dangerous. Vasu is devastated to know this and runs towards the gate to stop Aparna. The staff members try to stop Vasu, but he shouts Aparna's name loudly. He screams in a crying voice, "Please, stop! Don't do this."

As he approaches Aparna, she begins to tremble. Every particle of hers seems to dissolve into the air. The entire atmosphere there becomes still and melancholic. Vasu was unable to contain himself. Meanwhile, Raman arrives and takes Vasu back to the lab. Raman informs them that Aparna has left behind a code before leaving, which can be used to track her. We can again locate her live location.

Waking Up

On the other hand, The bell rings. At 4:00 in the morning, Aparna wakes up sleeping on the ninth day (nov., 2021) at the Upasana Center in Lucknow.

As Aparna wakes up, she surveys her surroundings with confusion. It takes her a moment to fully grasp the situation, but eventually, all the memories come flooding back to her. Despite this, she remains seated for a while, lost in thought. With no phone nearby and no one to ask, she is left to contemplate whether it was real or just a dream that she experienced.

Everyone must remain silent at the Upasana Center.

From 11.30 am to 12 o'clock Guruji stays in the hall for questions and answers. Before or after that, no one is allowed to talk to anyone.

Aparna was filled with restlessness now, as she recalled the time, she had witnessed a meditation teacher dozing off during a session. She had pondered over the fact that if such a person could become a teacher, anyone could. This thought lingered in her mind, and she wondered if she would get any help from that teacher. Yet, there was no one to talk to there so she decided to speak with him. Aparna was feeling like she is losing her mind.

As soon as the clock struck 11:30, Aparna hurriedly made her way to the teacher.

The teacher was sitting there with a smiley face. Before Aparna could say anything, the teacher asked her, "How was your trip to Alfa Earth?"

Aparna was very surprised and asked in amazement, "How do you know about my trip, and what is all this?"

"If I didn't know about your trip, how will I be your teacher?" He spoke.

The teacher chuckled, and at that moment, Aparna was reminded of the time when she had seen the teacher dozing off during a meditation session and had thought that anyone could become a teacher.

Aparna simply bowed down at that moment and said, "Please help me and tell me what is true and what is false. I feel like my mind will explode. I feel like I am going crazy. Where was I and where am I now? What is happening?"

The teacher smiled again and said, "Everything is true and everything is false. What is true for you is what you accept. What you do not know is false for you,".

Aparna and Guruji spoke for about half an hour, and towards the end of their conversation, Aparna shared that she did not know much, but just wanted to stay in a normal state and forget everything troubling her.

Guruji smiled and responded "remembering and forgetting are within our own control. We can choose to forget when we want to, and remember when we need to."

He even suggested that Aparna could forget their conversation if she wanted to. Upon hearing this, Aparna appeared lost in thought, perhaps pondering the power of her own mind.

After this, the meditation starts again. Aparna goes and sits on her seat. Guruji sits in front and guides her, "Focus on your breath first. Then gradually shift your attention to the sensations in your body."

Aparna forgets everything and just sits in meditation. As the night goes on, all her memories become hazy like a dream.

When Aparna woke up on the tenth day, her conscious memory of the event was not as clear as it is when we stay somewhere for a few days and remember everything. She only remembered that she had a dream, a long dream. That is, it. Everything else had slipped into her unconscious memory.

She did not even remember that she had already experienced the upcoming time once before.

On the tenth day in the evening, everyone returns their mobile phones at the meditation center. When Aparna's phone was returned to her, she immediately called Vijay.

At that time, Vijay was on a train from Delhi to Lucknow, and he was coming to pick up Aparna.

As soon as Vijay said, "You won't know where I am right now," Aparna replied, "Yes, you're on the train, right?"

As soon as Aparna said this, she felt a jolt in her body as if she had experienced it before. She felt déjà vu.

Vijay asked, "How did you know?"

Aparna hesitated a little and said, "Well, I just guessed it."

Aparna had resigned from her last job at that time and was in the notice period. So, she had planned to pack her things and return to Delhi from Lucknow. The next day, Aparna and Vijay went to Delhi.

Subsequently, Aparna's life remained unchanged. Everything unfolded in the same manner as before, and she found herself reliving the same life cycle once again. This time seemed familiar to her, yet nothing was retained in her conscious memory.

Upon arriving in Delhi, she joined the Future Bright Life Insurance Company. Four days after joining, the same two people, Ankur, and Sudhir, came as new members of the team. As soon as Aparna met Ankur and Sudhir, she felt déjà vu again. For a moment, she felt like she had already met them before. But then she ignored that feeling of déjà vu again.

Aparna shifted her home from Janakpuri to Paschim Vihar in the same way. Same sofa, same TV, same interior design, everything was done the same.

After that, in the month of February, the day came when Aparna consumed bhang in Mathura. On that day, Aparna had the longest Deja vu, which lasted for about five minutes. Aparna noticed that she remembered all the buildings and shops on her way.

As Aparna walked out of the building, she found herself repeating the same sentence she had just uttered moments before. In that instant, she suddenly remembered everything that was going to happen in the next five minutes. She recounted to Ankur and Sudhir that she had experienced this before, but they brushed it off as the effects of bhang. What followed was a tumultuous five minutes that turned into a three-day nightmare for Aparna. Eventually, she regained awareness of her own activity and her brain's response.

She was experiencing Deja vu repeatedly. All events occurred in the same sequence. Aparna's mother-in-law came to live with her.

They went to Mathura and Haridwar together. After sightseeing, they returned to Delhi, where Aparna became focused again on her meditation.

On March 16, 2022, Aparna wanted to meditate in her bedroom. Vijay was on his mobile phone, so she asked him to use earphones. Aparna began meditating at 10:00 pm and continued until late at night, while Vijay fell asleep. Despite not sleeping, Aparna's meditation allowed her to deepen her focus and concentration.

Her consciousness was gradually becoming more and more subtle, and in a short while, she found herself in emptiness.

It felt as if her mind had entered a dream, yet she remained conscious. When we dream, our logical thinking often fades away, that time Aparna was aware that she was experiencing a dream without logic.

She saw in her dream that many people were sitting and meditating in an open ground. The teacher who was sitting in front of them to guide them was Aparna's husband. She herself was also meditating there. While meditating, she was observing her feelings. She could feel her love and affection towards her husband. She had made up her mind to embrace consciousness and death. She was also talking to Lord Shiva in her thoughts during her meditation. She realized that she had been doing this for many days. She felt that all her energy was flowing from her head. As the energy was moving upwards, her body below was becoming lifeless.

The feeling was quite peaceful. It felt like she was merging with Lord Shiva. She turned into energy that rose from her head and suddenly felt a deep sense of love high up in the sky. Then, suddenly, she fell back down and onto her own head

While sitting in meditation on her bed, Aparna suddenly felt the energy rising from the top of her head. At the same time, her body experienced some movement. Like the previous time, something swirled from her stomach and rose towards her head. Suddenly, she felt that she was the wife of a spiritual master Jagat guru.

Aparna's realization was so deep that she forgot her identity for a few moments. When she opened her eyes, she found herself in the same way as before. Her t-shirt was soaked with tears, and she wondered how could so many tears come in just a few seconds.

Afterward, Aparna drifted off to sleep. Upon awakening, she felt as though she had spent the entire night conversing with someone, like her previous experience.

Beyond Control: Aparna's Surreal Experience

However, what happened next was something beyond anything Aparna had ever imagined. She sensed a wholly distinct entity within her own body as if she were suspended in mid-air. Through the eyes of this body, she could see, hear, and understand everything around her, yet she possessed no agency over any physical movement

Aparna was like a bystander, unable to speak or control her body. It felt like she was stuck inside her own body as if there were two versions of herself inside and outside at the same time. She realized that her body was not responding to her commands. It was as if she was watching a movie, with her body moving on its own. Even though she was standing in the kitchen making tea and talking to Vijay, it was her body that was doing all the actions, not Aparna.

Aparna became very restless when she saw this. It was as if she did not exist, yet she was alive. She was trapped inside her own body and did not know what to do. Everything was happening just like before. Aparna kept feeling that on the night she meditated, a ghost had taken control of her body.

In the beginning, the inner Aparna felt restless for almost a month. She was just floating in the air inside her own body. She had no control or power to take any action. She could only observe and see.

Aparna observed everything happening with her own eyes. However, during this time, she felt like she was experiencing Deja

Vu and would perform unusual movements. She decided to quit her decent job and went back home. This time, she felt like there was no inner voice guiding her. Despite this, all the events occurred just like they had happened before, just like when she had last gone to her hometown of Bhiwani. It was as if history was repeating itself.

Aparna did all those things almost exactly like the last time for about a week. She had the same argument with her family members as she had the last time.

One day, Aparna was sitting alone in her garden, thinking about life and what was happening to her. Then she experienced Deja Vu again. This time, the Deja Vu was equal for both her inner self and her outer self. They both felt that they had sat in this place before. This event had happened before. After this, Aparna's inner self became a little more alert.

She started observing each event very carefully. Besides watching and observing, she had nothing else. She could not do anything with her body, just feel from within. She could only sense it by being inside herself.

She did not know how long she would be trapped inside her own body like this. She was continuously praying to God that she did not want anything else, just control back over her body. If everything could just go back to how it was before, then she could make everything right again.

During this time, the mistakes she had made in her everyday life were now becoming apparent to Aparna.

When Aparna talked to her family, she listened carefully to every word she said before. She could feel how wrong she was. She kept thinking that once she regained control over her body, she would not want anything else. Aparna kept regretting that she had never valued what she had before

Aparna could see how much Aparna's family was worried about her. They were focused on making sure she ate well, drank enough water, and slept properly so that she could recover quickly. Aparna was observing her reactions from that time. She wanted to tell herself why she could not see her family's love. But she could not say anything.

After a few days, Aparna's condition deteriorated, and she began to realize that she was reliving her old life once again. She desperately tried to comprehend the reason behind this phenomenon. As the outside world kept Aparna occupied with her actions, the inner Aparna remained entangled in a web of her own thoughts.

The inside Aparna often observed that the outside Aparna was not active at all about her surroundings. Her elderly mother was washing clothes for her despite the pain in her feet, yet Aparna only made her do the work. She had never done anything for them to date. Seeing this, Aparna would get angry with herself many times.

Her younger sister cooks food for her. Her younger brother comes to ask about her well-being at least 10 times a day. Dad keeps hovering around. Upon seeing all this, the inside Aparna was getting very angry with herself. She was thinking inside that maybe this is the punishment for my bad deeds, that God is showing me my life again.

Aparna had come full circle in her life's journey, reliving it once again. As her master's voice became one with her, guiding her through meditation that night, she found herself back in that same moment. When she lay down to sleep that night, the same experience occurred, except this time there was no inner voice. Aparna drifted off to sleep in the usual way and awoke the next day without any unusual occurrences. While Aparna's inner journey had been remembered up to this point, her external self moved according to its own rhythm.

Trapped within her own body, Aparna was just pondering on what exactly had happened. If there was any inner voice at that time, where was it this time?

Completing The Cycle

The next day when Aparna woke up, everything was back to normal and she had regained control over her body. There was only one memory that was troubling her. But Aparna was very happy to have her body back. She wanted to tell someone about her story, but before that, her life had become so crazy that words were not enough to describe it. Therefore, she thought it was better not to tell anyone.

Aparna thanked Lord Shiva for that day and decided that she did not need to know anything beyond this. She just had to live her life. After this, life went back to its routine. Aparna started going to the office again. A few days later, Vijay also came back home.

After Vijay's return, Aparna wanted to make him feel special and loved. She decided to plan a warm welcome for him by ordering his favorite cake and some beautiful flowers. She also took the time to decorate their bedroom, making it cozy and inviting.

As the days passed, Aparna and Vijay found themselves settling into a comfortable routine. However, adjusting to a new life together was not without its challenges. Aparna and Vijay had to learn to navigate each other's quirks and habits, finding a balance that worked for both. They had to make compromises and sacrifices, but they were determined to make their relationship work.

As winter set in once again, Aparna found herself feeling content and happy. She was enjoying her life with Vijay, and she knew that they had a bright future ahead of them. Together, they were creating a life filled with love, warmth, and joy.

One night, Aparna had a dream in which she saw Vasu. The moment she laid eyes on him, Aparna felt an inexplicable connection with him. It was as if she had already spent a lifetime with Vasu. This dream sequence continued to play out in her subconscious, with Vasu appearing almost every night. They would explore new places together, or sometimes Vasu would woo Aparna with his romantic gestures. The memories of those moments spent with Vasu were etched into her unconscious mind, but Aparna couldn't seem to recall them in the present.

As the dreams persisted, Aparna began to feel increasingly disturbed. She found herself thinking about the dreams constantly, trying to make sense of their significance. These recurring dreams were causing her mental balance to waver, and Aparna was struggling to regain her composure.

Aparna had been experiencing vivid dreams of Vasu for some time, and they had been affecting her mental balance. She confided in Vijay, her partner, about her experiences, hoping that he would understand her. However, Vijay failed to see things from her perspective, which resulted in a heated argument between them. This repeated itself, and Aparna found it difficult to focus on her job as she was constantly preoccupied with her dreams and Vijay's inability to comprehend her.

To make matters worse, Vijay had to travel daily from Gurugram to Delhi to be with Aparna, which was becoming a burden. Aparna's restlessness grew as she continued to grapple with conflicting emotions about her devotion and marriage. She found it challenging to focus on her office work, which ultimately led to her resigning from her job within just six months.

Eventually, Vijay and Aparna decided to return to Delhi and start afresh. They left behind the troubles that plagued their relationship in Gurugram.

However, even after coming to Delhi, Aparna did not find peace in her life. Keeping her financial condition in mind, Aparna thought of joining a job again. This time, Vijay's office was next to their house. But Aparna's new office was quite far away now. She had to travel to Noida by metro for almost one and a half hours.

Aparna was grappling with the stress of her new job. Her boss, Rishi, had a notorious reputation for his unpleasant demeanor and was known to constantly apply additional pressure on his subordinates. Despite Aparna's impressive professional track record, she was struggling to cope with her current circumstances. Her recurring dreams and persistent feelings of déjà vu, coupled with the challenging nature of her hardcore field sales job, made her situation more daunting.

Rishi seemed to have taken a particular interest in Aparna, perhaps due to her remarkable performance history. However, this increased scrutiny only served to amplify Aparna's anxiety levels. With the weight of her responsibilities and the overwhelming work environment bearing down on her, Aparna found herself struggling to maintain her composure and retain her focus.

Along with the pressure of her new boss and job, Aparna's attention was also occupied by a story that consumed her day and night. It was a tale that had become a constant presence in her life.

Every day, Aparna would commute back home from work on the metro, just like any other day. But on this day, she found herself lost in thought, her mind completely absorbed in the story. As she sat there, her eyes grew heavy, and before she knew it, she had dozed off.

Suddenly, Aparna remembered everything that she had forgotten.

Aparna's mind was overwhelmed with memories of the past when she was with Vasu. It all came flooding back to her, the moments of joy, the moments of sadness, and the moments of love. She remembered how she had embarked on a journey to Alfa Earth, a planet full of mysteries and wonders, and how she had eventually returned to the Upasana center through her connection with Nemo.

Despite all these memories, Aparna still could not recollect what she had seen during her connection with Nemo. It was as if a piece of the puzzle was still missing, and she could not put everything together. She could not recall what had happened to her during that time or what she had experienced. The feeling of not knowing haunted her, and she could not help but wonder what had transpired during her connection with Nemo.

Once again, Aparna was left feeling confused and lost. She could not help but think about her entire story, the experiences she had lived through, and yet, she had nothing in her hand to show for it. All she had were fragmented memories and a feeling of unease. She wondered if she would ever be able to make sense of it all and find her true purpose.

Aparna resolved to return to the Upasana center and speak with the same meditation teacher. When she confided in Vijay about her decision, he became angry and insisted that she see a doctor again. Although Aparna considered the possibility that Vijay was right, her medical reports came back normal after her second consultation.

Despite taking medication for a week, Aparna's memory remained unrecovered. Regardless, she still went to the same center in Lucknow after an argument with Vijay, without any concern. However, upon arriving, she discovered that the meditation teacher she had spoken with was not present. Seeking reassurance, Aparna inquired about other people's experiences with meditation, but each person had a different response. Faced with no other solution, Aparna concluded that she had no choice but to go to the Jagatguru. so, she planned to visit the famous Shiva temple the following week, where it is believed that visitors are relieved of any spirits or occult issues, she returned to Delhi at that time.

Journey To Remembrance

Aparna visits the famous ashram of Jagat Guru in the south on a weekend. Aparna begins her journey by visiting the Shiva temple, where she sits and meditates for nearly 5 hours. As she meditates, her focus deepens, and she begins to remember everything, including her connection to Nemo.

She remembered Nemo had told her about how on Alpha earth the primal energy of nature, was disturbed because people were not living in harmony with nature. He showed her how Vasu's body had other possibilities of Vasu traveling in it and fulfilling their desires, which caused an imbalance in nature. Nemo had also taught her about the principle of birth and death in nature and how everyone had to pay the price for disturbing this principle.

Upon learning this, Aparna suddenly felt a decrease in her affection toward Vasu.

Afterward, Nemo showed her the essence of life by taking her on a tour of the entire universe. Aparna saw the unity and interconnectedness of all things, and she felt a deep sense of belongingness. She realized that there were only two types of energies in the universe, male and female and that these energies were the fundamental building blocks of the universe. She realized that every individual was anexpression of these two energies in different proportions and that at their core, they are the same.

Through Nemo, she understood the entire illusion. Nemo had taken Aparna to a state of mind where nothing mattered, where everything was just as it should be. In this state, there was no right or wrong, no good or bad. There was no mine or yours, no ownership or possession. Aparna was able to exist in the bodies of all the creatures in the universe, and she was able to feel life itself. It was a state of meditation where there was no distinction between your body and mine. Aparna was able to see herself in everything and everyone around her. She could feel the energy that flowed through her and all living things. She could sense the interconnectedness of everything and everyone.

Aparna had heard Vasu talk about other dimensions many times, and she was curious to learn more. Nemo took Aparna to a dimension where she could see the inhabitants of Earth. The entire planet appeared in black and white, and all creatures were simply energy patterns. Aparna saw that no one was eating or drinking, nor were they talking to each other. Everyone was simply wandering around the barren and desolate earth. Each creature had its own world in its mind, and the entire planet was moving according to its perceptions. Every world was interconnected, and everything was part of a greater consciousness.

As their meditation session came to an end, Nemo posed a question to Aparna – "If you were to take Mahasamadhi, how would you integrate yourself into the universe we just witnessed?"

It was a test of Aparna's understanding of the universe and her place in it.

Aparna thought for a moment and then replied, "I will die like a mother. I will become a protective wall for all living beings, wherever and whenever they need me."

And with those words, something incredible happened. Aparna's body dissolved into tiny particles, and she became one with the universe. She had reached a state of pure love and oneness with all things. As she merged with the universe, she felt herself becoming Shiva, the highest form of expression of love. It was an unforgettable experience that transformed Aparna's perception of the world and left her forever changed.

After that, Aparna finally opened her eyes in the Jagatguru Shiva's temple after 6 hours. She realized that she had expended a great deal of energy in trying to rewind her memories and now she was feeling completely exhausted. Her mind was in a state of turmoil as it struggled to make sense of everything, she had experienced. She lay down on the ground, trying to catch her breath and regain her composure. It was as if she had run a marathon, and now her body was screaming for rest. She closed her eyes and focused on her breathing, trying to slow it down and calm her mind.

Through this experience, Aparna came to understand the entire illusion. She realized that the world around her was not what it appeared to be. The things she thought were important no longer held the same value. She was able to let go of her ego and embrace the present moment fully.

After a few minutes she stepped outside, and her eyes fell upon a large peepal tree. She noticed that the Jagatguru had used some occult technique to bind a few spirits with an iron chain around the tree. Aparna could not see anything when she entered the temple, but as soon as she stepped outside, she could feel the impact of her meditation experience, she was not afraid at that moment, her motherly emotions were running high, and she felt a divine presence guiding her. Without hesitation, Aparna approached the peepal tree and gently touched its trunk with love and compassion. Suddenly, all the spirits were released, and She realized that her spiritual journey was not over yet and that she had much more to explore. Now she knew that whatever obstacles she might face in the future, she could overcome them with love, compassion, and the divine guidance that was always with her.

After coming outside, Aparna decided to quench her thirst by having a glass of refreshing mixed fruit juice. The coolness of the juice helped to soothe her exhausted body, and the blend of fruity flavors was a treat for her taste buds. Aparna enjoyed the sweet and tangy taste of the juice, and it helped to rejuvenate her energy levels. She felt grateful for the small pleasures in life and savored every sip of the delicious juice. Aparna did not feel the urge to meet Jagatguru. Instead, she left the temple and immediately headed towards the main city to find a hotel. She had a flight scheduled for the next day and wanted to get some rest before that.

The day had been overwhelming for her, with her memories flooding back and encountering occult practices at the temple. She needed some time to process everything that had happened and regain her energy. She found a cozy hotel and checked in, hoping for a good night's sleep.

Reunion With Vasu: Aparna's Second Chance?

Other side Vasu had been searching for Aparna for a long time now. He had tried every possible way to contact her, but all his efforts went in vain.

Finally, Vasu was able to connect with Aparna in her dream state, where she was semi-conscious. Aparna had already known everything and was determined to make Vasu realize that she would not live with him this time.

The next day, she woke up and headed to the airport, knowing that Vasu wanted her to leave her body. She continued to make efforts to return to Delhi. As she sat in her seat on the plane, she silently prayed to Shiva. But as the flight took off, Aparna felt all her energy leaving her body, and she became unconscious. She felt as if she was dying.

And now she was here, in Vasu's lab. Aparna looked at Vasu and realized that he had been the one who had brought her here.

Vasu spoke softly, "I am sorry, Aparna. I know you had your own plan, but I could not let you go."

Aparna did not say anything. She just lay there, staring at the ceiling, lost in her own thoughts.

After a few moments, Aparna slowly got up from the bed and looked at Vasu, and said in a firm voice "Thank you for bringing me here, Vasu. But now I need to go back to Delhi and face the consequences of my actions. Vasu, you need to understand that my karmic impressions are still incomplete with Vijay on Earth, and now it is time for you to leave Alpha Earth. This is not the right time for us. We will meet again after my life ends on Earth. You must accept the time and the need for it. Your grandfather is waiting for you on the next plane of existence. This is the time when you need to become a guide and protector of your world."

Vasu said, "But how can you go back? Your body is dead there, you died there."

Aparna smiled and placed her hand on Vasu's cheek and said, "So this time, I am your master, by the way." After that, she simply sat in a meditative state with closed eyes, chanted "Om Namah Shivay," and left. Her body became unconscious there.

Vasu was left alone with Aparna's lifeless body, feeling overwhelmed and confused. He could not understand what had just happened, but he knew that Aparna was gone. As he sat there, he realized that she had been right - their time together on Alfa Earth was over, and it was time for him to move on and fulfill his destiny as a Nemo.

Other side Aparna woke up at the Delhi airport sitting alone on a bench with empty hands. She had no mobile phone or luggage with her. She stepped outside and used a security guard's phone to call Vijay. Vijay had already come to the airport to pick her up. When he saw Aparna, became angry and scolded her for being so careless as to lose her belongings at the airport.

Aparna listened silently as Vijay lectured her, and they both returned home. After arriving home, Vijay continued to scold Aparna for her carelessness, but Aparna remained silent. That day, even during Vijay's anger, Aparna could see the scared child within him.

That night, as she lay in bed, she could not help but laugh as she remembered her entire experience. She also recalled the teachings of her meditation teacher, who had told her that remembering or forgetting was in her own hands, like a touch that could be forgotten or remembered when needed.

Connecting Dots

She remembered that the teacher said "As human beings, we are born into this world without any knowledge or understanding of our surroundings. It is only through the guidance of our parents and the people around us that we begin to learn about the world we live in. We are told who our parents are, what our name is, and what the things around us are called. We accept these things without question, trusting that the information we are given is true. As we grow older, we begin to learn about the rules and norms of our society. We are taught what is right and wrong, what is good and bad.

We adapt to these rules, and they become a part of our identity. We may even begin to believe that they are an inherent part of who we are. But the question remains, do we really know where we are right now, and what is real and what is fake in our surroundings? Is our perception of the World based on what we have been taught, or is there a deeper truth that we have yet to discover?

Perhaps the most important question is whether we have anything that truly belongs to us in this world. Have we formed our own beliefs and values, or have we simply adopted those of our society? Do we have a sense of purpose and identity that is uniquely our own, or are we simply following the path that has been laid out for us?

These are questions that each of us must ask ourselves as we navigate our way through life. It is only by questioning our assumptions and beliefs that we can begin to discover our true selves and our place in the world.

As human beings, we tend to get caught up in the details of our lives, analyzing every little thing and trying to make sense of it all. But in doing so, we often forget that life is meant to be lived.

We forget to take a step back and appreciate the bigger picture, the journey that we are all on.

The journey of life is a spiritual one, and the experiences that we have along the way are just a trailer for what is to come. We are all on this journey together, coming from somewhere and going somewhere. The destination may be unknown, but the journey itself is what matters most.

It is important to remember that everything that we see, hear, taste, and experience is a creation of our own minds. We are the creators of our own reality, and we have the power to choose how we experience the world around us.

As we navigate through life, we should embrace every opportunity to experiment with what we feel like, to choose our own right and wrong. Whatever has happened in the past, whatever is happening now, and whatever will happen in the future – all of it is right. Every experience is a lesson and every lesson is a part of our spiritual journey.

It can be easy to feel small and insignificant in the grand scheme of things, but we must remember that we are all a part of creation. We are both a tiny part of the whole and the creators of our own reality. This is what we should learn from our journey – that we can shape our own lives and our own reality. So let us live our journey to the fullest, embracing every experience and learning from every lesson along the way.

Aparna's entire so-called spiritual journey had given her a new perspective on life.

Aparna fell asleep that night while reminiscing about everything that had been said.

The following day, Aparna went to her office and headed straight to her boss, Rishi, to submit her resignation. Rishi was taken aback and could not believe what he was seeing.

He said, "I knew from the beginning that you do not deserve this job. You are not capable enough to handle it."

Aparna smiled and replied, "Dear sir, you are not the judge of my life. Your behavior of threatening people in their day-to-day lives is not a great way to do your work. You judged me too quickly without getting to know me. But let me tell you something, I feel sorry for managers like you who intimidate those who work under them in small offices. If you had trusted me, I could have been an asset to your team. But thankfully, I have come to understand what life truly means."

With those words, Aparna left the office and headed out on a new journey in her life.

She had decided to take control of her life and make her own choices. She realized that she did not need to rely on someone else's opinion of her abilities and capabilities. Instead, she was going to trust herself and take a leap of faith toward new opportunities. This was the beginning of a new chapter in her life, one where she was the author of her own story.

Aparna decided to never regret anything in her life and to go with the ebbs and flows of life. She began focusing on all the desires she had always wanted to fulfill but never acted upon. She started to notice the gaps in her life and what she needed to do to fill them. Aparna realized that she could become anything she wanted, whether it was a yoga teacher, a founder of a teaching academy, or the creator of a new cosmetic brand. She had always dreamed of starting a company called "Mud me more" where she could produce natural face packs, mud masks, and bathing powders. Aparna could even become an author, writing about the experiences that had shaped her life. But most importantly, Aparna decided that she would not cry anymore. She would embrace the highs and lows of life, enjoying the flow of her emotions. She had found the courage to grab life by the horns, take control of her own destiny, and follow her passions.

Aparna had finally found her momentum, and she was determined to make the most of it. She knew that the journey would be difficult, but she was ready for it. She was ready to take risks, learn from her mistakes, and grow from her experiences. And as she began her new journey, she felt free and alive for the first time in a long time.